Finished reading 5-1-2019

JOY IN THE COVENANT

Reflections by

JULIE B. BECK

Foreword by Clayton M. Christensen

DESERET
BOOK

SALT LAKE CITY, UTAH

Image on page 1 © Shaiith/Shutterstock; page 61 © Subbotina Anna/Shutterstock; page 99 © nobelio/Shutterstock. Olive branch on chapter opening pages © Sandra_M/Shutterstock.

Visit us at deseretbook.com

Library of Congress Cataloging-in-Publication Data

Names: Beck, Julie B., author.
Title: Joy in the covenant / Julie B. Beck.
Description: Salt Lake City, Utah : Deseret Book, [2018] | Includes bibliographical references and index.
Identifiers: LCCN 2018028056 | ISBN 9781629724683 (hardbound : alk. paper)
Subjects: LCSH: Christian life—Mormon authors. | The Church of Jesus Christ of Latter-day Saints—Doctrines. | Mormon Church—Doctrines.
Classification: LCC BX8656 .B425 2018 | DDC 248.4/89332—dc23
LC record available at https://lccn.loc.gov/2018028056

Printed in the United States of America
Publishers Printing, Salt Lake City, UT

10   9   8   7   6   5   4   3   2   1

CONTENTS

Foreword. v

Acknowledgments vii

IDENTITY

  1. A Joyful Covenant 3

  2. We Know Who We Are! 10

  3. Acorns, Oak Trees, and a Front-Row Seat 18

  4. Glad Tidings of Truth 31

  5. An Amazing Gift 43

PURPOSE

  6. Learning from Experience: Lessons from Blinker Lights,
     Spare Change, and Bologna Sandwiches. 63

  7. Tender Trials and Assuring Answers 76

  8. Pioneers, Promises, and Planting: Evidence of Faith,
     Assurance of Hope 82

CONTENTS

Joyful Labor

9. Living a Fruitful Life 101
10. "Somebody" Has a Name 110
11. Hearing the Lord's Voice 116
12. Why We Are Organized into Quorums
    and Relief Societies 126
13. "Let My Life Be Music" 145
14. What Is Our Mission? 156

    Index 163

FOREWORD
Clayton M. Christensen

I'm delighted to be able to write a foreword for Sister Beck's marvelous book, which should be required reading for every member of the Church. I will introduce it by first discussing an experience in my life that happened in parallel with the experiences she details here.

Many years ago, I "called myself" on a lifelong mission to build the kingdom of God. Up until that time, I believed all the good things of our faith. I had taught the principles and doctrine to the people in Korea. And then a few years later, while studying at Oxford, I came to a point in my life when I needed to know, without any doubt, if it was true. And if it was true, I promised I would give my life to the Lord. I have shared this experience in *The Power of Everyday Missionaries* and in various talks because it changed the course of my life.

Reading Sister Beck's thoughts here, I have realized that I not only found out that the Book of Mormon and The Church of Jesus Christ of Latter-day Saints was true, but God also showed me my identity. He revealed to me that He knows me personally, and had a work for me to do.

Since those midnight hours in Oxford, I have had two callings—the ones given to me by my priesthood leaders, and the one God planted in me all those years ago. I have given my life to both of these callings. But the one God planted in me drives me. It gives me direction and a reason for doing all that I have been able to do.

My wife, Christine, and I have found great peace as we build in our corner of the world. Many of our joyful moments and relationships came to my mind as I read Sister Beck's words.

One thing I deeply appreciate about this wonderful book is how she teaches of *Identity, Purpose,* and *Joyful Labor* with power and boldness. It is that same strength we came to love when she served as the Relief Society General President. As she teaches, we learn more about how she came to that power and boldness. She describes being taught by her parents and observing the growth of the Church in Brazil, which makes her story unique.

When her mother wrote letters to members of the church in Brazil, all of her letters were signed with "*Cresceremos,*" meaning, "We will grow." This idea that we are driven to grow was instilled in everything they did. It's no coincidence that since that time, the church in Brazil has grown miraculously. And as Sister Beck teaches, it can be the same for us as well. Whether it is as a church, or as an individual disciple, we can grow by making and keeping covenants and helping others do the same. My only fear is that today, particularly within the church, many aren't focused on growth at all. We manage, we get by, or we administer this and that piece of the kingdom. But we don't have to simply manage our lives, or manage the church, or manage our homes. If we ask Him, God will show us how to truly grow.

Thus, for anyone who feels a desire to be "called to the work," I urge you to read this book. For anyone who is currently leading in a ward, stake, or family, or who wants to learn how to build the kingdom of God, I urge you to read this book. Just as I experienced, just as Sister Beck experienced, God is anxious for us to know personally what our identity and purpose are, so that when we work in building His Kingdom, He can pour out His blessings.

ACKNOWLEDGMENTS

The reflections in this book are personal expressions of deep-seated feelings and beliefs. I wrote them to increase the faith of my own posterity and the faith of others who might read them. They are, for the most part, previously unpublished. They are refined summaries of countless hours of study, thought, and writing. Each message was given in a unique setting to a unique group of people. In my preparation to give each message, I pondered who would be there, what they may need to hear, and, always, what the Lord would have me say to convey the thoughts and impressions of my heart. Each message has been revised to be appropriate for this book.

In these reflections, I draw heavily on the lives of my parents and the lessons I have learned from them. They were my first earthly teachers, and their examples formed the foundation for my faith.

Although I heard the words my parents taught and saw their examples, I needed a normal maturing process to assimilate those truths into my life. As my opportunities to study and teach the gospel have multiplied, I have found myself drawn to words and ideas my parents shared when I was a child—words that are comforting, reassuring, and faith promoting. From my parents I learned the importance of family—not just our own family but the family of God.

I thank my husband, Ramon, who pressed on with his own great goals while I studied, pondered, and wrote. Then he listened to me read my drafts and sat through my speeches. What a good sport with a great testimony! Our children have been magnificent counselors and have lifted me at all times.

Aaron West became my "friendly neighborhood editor" years ago and has had endless patience and wisdom in helping me smooth the rough edges of my words. He has been a faithful partner in the preparation of the book, and I have been blessed by his rare gift to enhance a writer's thoughts and be a tough critic without being tough.

Great appreciation goes to friends at Deseret Book: Sheri Dew, Laurel Day, Lisa Roper, and their production team, who were kind enough to think I could do this and then generous in guiding me through the process.

My deepest gratitude is reserved for my Heavenly Father and His Son, Jesus Christ, for Their endless kindness and awareness of each of us. My covenants with Them are the lodestar of my life and a joy and blessing.

IDENTITY

"How merciful is our God unto us, for
he remembereth the house of Israel, both
roots and branches; and he stretches forth
his hands unto them all the day long."

—Jacob 6:4

1

A Joyful Covenant

My father and mother, William Grant and Geraldine Hamblin Bangerter, enjoyed camping in tents, horse riding, fishing, and farming. They gained great satisfaction from singing around the campfire in their own backyard while roasting hotdogs and marshmallows. They enjoyed hard physical labor, such as mending fences, caring for animals, and making repairs on their farm. Mother dug in her garden with a pickax, not a hoe, because she said it was better exercise and made a bigger impact in the soil. Daddy built homes, meaning he cut boards and hammered nails and worked cement with his own hands. They also had great refinement. They hosted elegant dinner parties in their home, appreciated art and beauty, and were endlessly fascinated by people and places, geography and history. They were both scriptorians and loved to teach the gospel. I wrote the following message to summarize the legacy of faith they left me—their joyful approach to keeping covenants.

Mother was gifted in finding opportunities to teach in daily living. She rarely worked alone, and as we cooked or weeded or drove with her in the car, she asked inspired questions, shared stories of her childhood, and taught lessons she was learning from her scripture study.

Daddy would read aloud from his favorite novels or share captivating stories or lessons from the Bible and Book of Mormon as we straightened the house after dinner. We followed him, as if he were the pied piper, from room to room until the house was in order. If we grew too engrossed in his melodious voice and stopped our work to draw closer to him and hear better during the "exciting parts" of the stories, he would slowly close the book and say, with a twinkle in his eye, "I guess you don't want me to read any more . . ." After which we would feverishly begin folding the clothes or picking up the toys.

A FAMILY MOTTO

No experience demonstrates better my parents' approach to keeping covenants and becoming what the Lord wanted them to become than their response to being called to preside over the Brazilian Mission. At that time, in the summer of 1958, they lived near their own parents and siblings and enjoyed close friendships and family gatherings. We were a young and active family, and Mother was expecting child number seven. Daddy had been serving as stake president for about four years. Their construction business was doing well, and they had just moved into the new home they had built.

Then President Stephen L Richards, a Counselor in the First Presidency, asked Daddy and Mother to leave all that and serve in Brazil. In those days, there was no standard limit for the service of mission presidents. A call signaled a long-term commitment, and everything in our carefully ordered lives in Utah was disassembled. All our belongings were stored or given away, friends and family members hosted farewell parties, and my parents sold their home.

Mother recounted her experience of leaving home and getting established in Brazil:

"I felt the influence of the Lord helping us to cut the strings one by one and to make the preparations. And as we did so, my testimony about our mission grew stronger. I decided I would give my whole-hearted support to what was ahead of us. My eyes would be single to the Lord's purposes in Brazil.

"After a nineteen-hour flight from New York City, we arrived in São Paulo in a propeller airplane. It was the day before Thanksgiving in the United States. Our six children, ages one to thirteen, were soon engrossed in the differences between our old and our new countries. They were absolutely delighted with the old three-story mission home, which also served as Church headquarters in Brazil. Ten days after our arrival, our seventh child, Peggy Brasilia, was born.

"The excitement of seeing new things soon gave way to the realities of living. It was the rainy season. We had no washer, no dryer, and two children in diapers. When the sun came out, the flies came in because there were no screens on our windows. The upstairs bathroom plumbing dripped conveniently into a pan in our dining room, and the plumber helped by making a hole in the ceiling with his brace and bit so the water didn't drip—it ran out instead. Our children were fighting skin infections from scratching bug bites and there was no vacuum to keep the carpet clean. Trying to arrange simple household matters seemed futile when I knew only a few Portuguese words.

"After several weeks of domestic hardship, I awoke to another drizzling day and no dry diapers. My courage gave way, and I hurried to my room, buried my face in the pillow, and cried a cloudburst of tears.

"I was in the middle of my private storm when Grant made his untimely appearance. Thrilled to be back where he had served his mission seventeen years earlier, he had barely been able to control his exuberance. To him, it seemed there had been no problems!

"'Why, what's the matter?' he asked, looking shocked.

"Through my sobs I explained all the difficulties. I thought he would put his arms around me and offer his understanding and sympathy, but instead he began to roar with laughter. Gleefully he pulled me out onto the veranda, where we stood in the drizzle. Waving his arm, he asked me to look out on the horizon. 'Look at the green foliage contrasted against the red earth, and the tall buildings silhouetted against the sky,' he said. 'Where would you see anything more beautiful?'

"In that moment I did not see what he saw. I looked and for an instant, I thought I saw the Rocky Mountains. I was homesick.

"Aware that he was not helping me much, Grant took me back inside. He put both hands on my shoulders, looked straight into my eyes, and said, 'I know that you are experiencing some hardships, but one of the exciting parts of going to a new country is learning the language. You'll soon learn it! We'll find a vacuum and get the washer fixed. You are a nurse and will find something to take care of the children's skin infections. Someday, when we go back to the United States, you'll want to tell people about your interesting times here. And when you do, you and they will laugh about your challenges. Why wait until then to enjoy it? Enjoy it now!'

"I felt as if someone had raised the curtain on the second act of a play. I caught the wisdom of my husband's words, and I began to laugh. 'You're right,' I said. 'We *should* enjoy it now!'

"And so we shared several lighthearted, rejuvenating minutes and, together, began enjoying 'the second act.'

"This philosophy so influenced our attitudes that nothing could discourage us. When daily adversities came—like discovering that our water was turned off, missing an airplane, or learning that my car had been impounded—we would just look at each other and say 'Enjoy it!' and laugh. The entire mission felt the reverberations as they adopted our philosophy and changed many a bewildering situation into a happy one."[1]

After returning to the United States from Brazil in 1963, we started over with our lives. By then, the family had grown to include nine children. The tenth child arrived a couple of years later. Daddy had to launch a new business. My parents had to find a home and struggle to reestablish themselves financially. One daughter was attending a university, and a son was preparing to serve a mission. And Mother and Daddy continued working as hard as ever to serve the Lord.

"Enjoy It!" became a family motto. It turned into shorthand for looking at life as a school, a time given to us to improve ourselves, to keep covenants, and to help the Lord with His work.

STAYING ON THE COVENANT-KEEPING PATH

In Jacob chapter 5, we read an allegory about the covenant family of the Lord. The allegory centers on an involved process undertaken by the master of the vineyard to refine the fruit of tame and wild olive trees. In the allegory, the master of the vineyard intends to harvest, to gather unto himself the fruits of his labors, and he wants the fruit to be good, not bitter or corrupt. The master works diligently and with his might to preserve the trees and the fruit. In order to do so, he oversees a process of pruning and grafting to produce the "most precious fruit." The lord of the vineyard and the servant who works with him nurture and care for the trees and preserve the precious roots. The concern of the master of the vineyard is that he might lose his trees, that the roots might die. When we consider that the roots, the life-giving force of the trees, represent covenants, then we see how important covenants are. We can learn a great deal from Jacob 5 about how the Lord sees His covenant family. As we make and keep covenants with the Lord, He purifies us. Bit by bit, we become new people who are more like Him. At the end of the allegory, the master rejoices in his "fruit," which is "most precious unto him."[2]

Our Lord has established His covenant and His people, and in each generation that covenant is renewed. President Russell M. Nelson has counseled us to "begin with the end in mind." In his first message as President of the Church, he said, "The end for which each of us strives is to be endowed with power in a house of the Lord, sealed as families, faithful to covenants made in a temple that qualify us for the greatest gift of God, that of eternal life." He also counseled: "Keep on the covenant path. Your commitment to follow the Savior by making covenants with Him and then keeping those covenants will open the door to every spiritual blessing and privilege available to men, women, and children everywhere."[3] We continue to keep our covenants by helping others—nurturing and diligently laboring in the vineyard to "prepare the way, that [the Lord] may bring forth again the natural fruit, which natural fruit is good and the most precious above all other fruit."[4] In June 2018, President Nelson said: "Every child of our Heavenly Father deserves the opportunity to *choose* to follow Jesus Christ, to accept and receive His gospel with all of its blessings—yes, all the blessings that God promised to the lineage of Abraham, Isaac, and Jacob, who, as you know, is also known as Israel. . . . *Anytime* you do *anything* that helps *anyone*—on either side of the veil—take a step toward making covenants with God and receiving their essential baptismal and temple ordinances, you are helping to gather Israel. It is as simple as that."[5]

My parents demonstrated their joy in keeping their covenants through their daily acts and teachings and in their fruitful lives. They carried with them a spirit of enjoyment, which influenced how they taught us. They had knowledge of their identity, their purpose, and their sacred responsibility to labor with the Lord to bring about a harvest of faith in us. From them I learned of the Lord's covenant, the Abrahamic covenant, which binds us to Him. From them I learned of the power behind that covenant. Through their influence, I felt the first stirrings of the security and confidence that come from knowing my identity and purpose as a daughter of God and the importance of being a full participant in all the blessings He has to offer. From my parents I learned that I can be one of the Lord's covenant children, that I was precious to Him in the beginning and that my value to Him is beyond price.

In our family, it was understood that we would do our best to learn from and try to enjoy the growth we acquired from overcoming challenges. Our parents knew that some experiences and seasons in life are particularly stretching, and they always encouraged us to remember who we were and to summon faith to keep getting up after defeats or difficulties. If we wrote or called to tell them how tough life was, they would remind us to enjoy the experience we were having. That counsel continued throughout our lives and helped to give us perspective. One day when I was new in my calling as Relief Society General President, my mother came to my office. She had a gift for me. As she handed it to me, she said, "I thought it was time you put this on your desk." I opened the gift. It was a sign that read, "Enjoy It!"

NOTES

1. Geraldine Hamblin Bangerter, "'Enjoy It!'" *Ensign,* June 1991, 45.
2. Jacob 5:74.
3. "A Message from the First Presidency, January 16, 2018," 3; available at https://www.lds.org/bc/content/ldsorg/church/news/2018/01/19/2018-01-1000-a-message-from-the-first-presidency.pdf; accessed 11 April 2018.
4. Jacob 5:61.
5. Russell M. Nelson, "Hope of Israel," Worldwide Youth Devotional, June 3, 2018, 6, 8.

2

WE KNOW WHO WE ARE!

In the summer of 2016, the sun shone on my oldest granddaughter and me as we enjoyed a happy visit outside our small camping trailer in a canyon near my home. She had decided to serve a mission, and she asked me what I suggested she study to help her prepare. We talked about scriptures she could read and practical skills to work on. Then we began talking about her preparation to enter the temple to make covenants for eternity, and we had a sweet discussion about her identity in a covenant family, the house of Israel. Our learning was so meaningful to us that we both felt it would be appropriate to share with sisters in my stake at a Relief Society event, which was held that September.

One evening Daddy began our family home evening lesson by singing part of a song he had heard as a World War II pilot: "We are poor little lambs who have lost our way. Baa, baa, baa!"[1] He then took us to the first chapter of Alma—about Nehor, an anti-Christ who taught some ideas that were new to the members of the Church at that time. Among other things, Nehor proclaimed that regardless of how they lived their lives, everyone would be saved in the end and that they "need not fear nor tremble" because the Lord had created every-one and would redeem everyone. Nehor became a "popular" preacher, and people gave him money to teach things that were easy for them to hear and live and that did not require them to keep covenants or be accountable to God for their actions.[2]

On other occasions, my father warned us of other false teachings we needed to avoid so that we would not be "poor little lambs who have lost our way." He taught us about Korihor, another anti-Christ, who borrowed some ideas from Nehor. Korihor exploited many philosophies that are still taught today, although they are often pre-sented to us as new, innovative, and liberating. He taught a skeptical philosophy, saying that no one could verify prophecies concerning Christ because "ye cannot know of things which ye do not see." He manipulated thought and scorned faith by declaring that looking for-ward to a remission of sins was "the effect of a frenzied mind," caused by the "traditions of [the people's] fathers." He promoted the concepts of competition and survival of the fittest—that "every man fared in this life according to the management of the creature" and "prospered according to his genius." He blighted hope by declaring that "when a man was dead, that was the end thereof." His teachings must have been effective, because he led "away the hearts of many, causing them to lift up their heads in their wickedness."[3]

Those teachings are found in the "-isms" and "-ologies" of our day, and they continue to be effective. An increasing inventory of individ-uals, groups, and classifications incessantly clamor for an ever-greater share of our attention, and they lead many people to question their belief in God and become confused about their true identity.

The Lord has said that in our day, "the whole earth shall be in commotion, and men's hearts shall fail them."[4] However, He also says, "Be not troubled, for, when all these things shall come to pass, ye may know that the promises which have been made unto you shall be ful-filled."[5] In a world awash with false and confusing philosophies, we can find peace in the assurance of our enduring identity.

AN ETERNAL IDENTITY

Because of the restored gospel of Jesus Christ, we know that we are spirit children of heavenly parents[6] and that we "received [our] first lessons in the world of spirits and were prepared to come forth in the due time of the Lord to labor in his vineyard for the salvation of the souls of men."[7]

Each of us is a unique child of God, with an individual, divine identity. When we are baptized, we also gain a family identity. We become part of the covenant family of our Father in Heaven, the house of Israel, called to assist in the work of our Savior, Jesus Christ.

We trace this family identity to Abraham and his wife Sarah, who covenanted with God, as did Enoch and Noah and Adam and Eve before them. The Lord blessed Abraham to "be a father of many nations"[8] and Sarah to "be a mother of nations."[9] When the Lord established His covenant with them, He said that He would make Abraham "exceeding fruitful"[10] and that He would be "their God."[11] He said that this covenant was not just for them but for their "seed after [them] in their generations."[12] Their son Isaac and his wife Rebekah were given these same promises, which continued through their son Jacob, whose name the Lord changed to Israel. Jehovah, the premortal Jesus Christ and the God of our ancient fathers and mothers, gave laws and commandments—all part of a covenant tied to a family identity. His covenant empowered and blessed all who were faithful to Him.

This covenant continues today in the restored Church of Jesus Christ. In the Kirtland Temple, a heavenly messenger named Elias visited Joseph Smith and Oliver Cowdery. "Elias appeared," Joseph said, "and committed the dispensation of the gospel of Abraham, saying that in us and our seed all generations after us should be blessed."[13] President Joseph Fielding Smith taught, "Everything that pertains to that dispensation, the blessings that were conferred upon Abraham, the promises that were given to his posterity, all had to be restored, and Elias, who held the keys of that dispensation, came."[14]

When we are baptized, we "opt in" to receive those promises. We choose to become part of Heavenly Father's covenant family. As we make and keep our covenants, we receive the blessings and obligations given to Abraham and Sarah and to Isaac and Jacob and their families.

This Abrahamic covenant is our identity: a solid, unchanging belonging to a sacred family pedigree. This knowledge is supporting and reassuring. Our identity does not change as we transition through our life experience. It is not altered by being married or single, old or young, wealthy or destitute. It does not change with world conditions, with social swings, or with public opinion. It is an eternal identity that gives rich meaning and focus to our lives.

Teachings about this family identity can be found in all the scriptural witnesses of Christ—in the Old Testament, the New Testament, the Book of Mormon, the Doctrine and Covenants, the Pearl of Great Price, and current prophetic teachings. And when we receive a patriarchal blessing, we are told of our identity within the family of Abraham and Sarah and our ancestry in the house of Israel. As we study these teachings and learn more about God's covenant with His people, we see how He blesses those who honor Him.

The best place to learn about the rich and encompassing blessings of this covenant family is the temple. When we go to the temple and truly pay attention, we can learn that we are the fulfillment of Isaiah's prophecy: "Many people shall go and say, Come ye, and let us go up to the mountain of the Lord, to the house of the God of Jacob; and he will teach us of his ways, and we will walk in his paths."[15]

RESPONSIBILITIES OF THE HOUSE OF ISRAEL

When we make covenants, we accept clear responsibilities. I have learned that as members of The Church of Jesus Christ of Latter-day Saints, we are a called people. We are sent here for a purpose. We are under obligation to participate with the Savior in His work of salvation. This work makes it possible for everyone to be linked to God's covenant family if they so desire. For this reason, we send missionaries to share the gospel. For this reason, every member is also under obligation to share that message. We do not baptize people into the Lord's covenant merely to swell the membership of the Church. To all of Heavenly Father's children, we offer the opportunity to be part of His covenant family. We share the good news that our identity is eternal and that we can all be heirs with the Savior in our Father's blessings.[16] The Lord has commanded, "Thou shalt preach the fulness of my gospel, which I have sent forth in these last days, the covenant which I have sent forth to recover my people, which are of the house of Israel."[17]

For this same reason, we work to identify our ancestral family members who have died without receiving the ordinances of salvation, and we go to holy temples to receive those ordinances in their behalf. In the spirit world, they may choose to be full partakers of God's covenant.

We also have important saving work to do in our homes and families. We have the responsibility to teach children and grandchildren to be covenant makers and covenant keepers. Taking care of our families is sacred, important work, no less important than missionary work or temple work. Teaching and preparing every new generation is essential to secure an unbroken line of family covenant keeping.

But the daily needs of life press on all of us. We go to work; we cook, clean, feed, clothe, teach, and care for family members—those who are young and those who are old. It is the duty of parents to preside over, provide for, and protect their families and to nurture them in all that will lift and foster strength in them.

Our service as members of the house of Israel is not a checklist of things to do. It is not a race, nor is it a competition to see how much each of us can do. In the house of Israel, all faithful efforts count, and so we labor in the times and places we are needed and with the people who need us most. We often speak of missionaries as being in the field of labor. If we are keeping covenants and serving as members of the house of Israel, in whatever capacity, we are all "in the field." No office or service in church assignments and in our communities is superior or inferior, and no effort toward salvation is too small to please the Lord. The Apostle Paul referred to the Church as "the body of Christ"[18] and taught that we all have important roles to fulfill. He said, "By one Spirit are we all baptized into one body, whether we be Jews or Gentiles, whether we be bond or free; and have been all made to drink into one Spirit. For the body is not one member, but many."[19]

We can be at peace with ourselves and our contributions when we do all we can to bless our Father's children, especially those in our own families.

A GREAT FAITH-BASED WORK

As heirs to promised blessings, we are participating in a faith-based work. It is the power of our faith in Heavenly Father and Jesus Christ and in our covenants that carries us beyond our limited capacity and enables us to seek and receive miracles in our lives. The day of miracles has not ceased.[20]

Because we are human, it is a challenge to fulfill all the responsibilities that are laid upon us. We are imperfect and limited mortals, bound by time, weakness, exhaustion, discouragement, and restricted capacity. Therefore, we depend on the Savior, who carried out His infinite Atonement so He could increase our capacity to do His will. He knew us before we were born, and He prepared us to do specific work on His behalf.[21] It is His mission to help us succeed.

Through the prophet Joel, the Lord prophesied of our day. "I will pour out my spirit upon all flesh," He said. "And your sons and your daughters shall prophesy, your old men shall dream dreams, your young men shall see visions: and also upon the servants and upon the handmaids in those days will I pour out my spirit."[22]

The house of Israel was scattered anciently, and in our day that family is being gathered into God's covenant. The Lord declared, "And even so will I gather mine elect from the four quarters of the earth, even as many as will believe in me, and hearken unto my voice."[23] He promised, "I have a great work laid up in store, for Israel shall be saved, and I will lead them withersoever I will, and no power shall stay my hand."[24] "And righteousness and truth will I cause to sweep the earth as with a flood, to gather out mine elect from the four quarters of the earth."[25]

We do not need to be "poor little lambs who have lost our way." We gain a powerful family identity when we become part of God's covenant. As we stay true to His covenant, we receive blessings from heaven. And we enjoy the privilege of assisting the Lord in His work of salvation—participating in a tremendous faith-based effort to gather souls, His most precious fruit, into His covenant.

Notes

1. This line comes from Rudyard Kipling's poem "Gentlemen-Rankers." It was later parodied in "The Whiffenpoof Song." My father learned a version of the song when he was serving in the United States Air Force. See whiffenpoofs.com/about-us and kiplingsociety.co.uk/poems _gentlemen.htm; accessed 11 April 2018.
2. See Alma 1:3–5.
3. Alma 30:15–18.
4. Doctrine and Covenants 45:26.
5. Doctrine and Covenants 45:35.
6. See "The Family: A Proclamation to the World," *Ensign*, Nov. 2010, 129.
7. Doctrine and Covenants 138:56.
8. Genesis 17:4.
9. Genesis 17:16.
10. Genesis 17:6.
11. Genesis 17:8.
12. Genesis 17:9.
13. Doctrine and Covenants 110:12.
14. Joseph Fielding Smith, *Teachings of Presidents of the Church: Joseph Fielding Smith* (2013), 155.
15. Isaiah 2:3.
16. See Romans 8:16–17.
17. Doctrine and Covenants 39:11.
18. 1 Corinthians 12:27.
19. 1 Corinthians 12:13–14.
20. See Moroni 7:35–37.
21. See Jeremiah 1:5–10.
22. Joel 2:28–29.
23. Doctrine and Covenants 33:6.
24. Doctrine and Covenants 38:33.
25. Moses 7:62.

3

ACORNS, OAK TREES, AND
A FRONT-ROW SEAT

I still say prayers in Portuguese, and our grandchildren always sing "happy birthday" with us in that language at our birthday celebrations. The young ones seem perplexed when I tell them that when I was their age, I was speaking fluently in two languages. In our mission home in São Paulo, missionaries shared our evening meals. My siblings and I made a habit of pestering them in the mission office, asking if we could staple papers or run errands to help in any small way. We adored our missionary elders and sisters and wanted to be like them. Instead of playing "school" or "house," we would dress up in discarded missionary garb, scribble our own tracts, and go desk to desk in the mission office with our "door approach." Since we had a baptismal font in our backyard, we frequently attended baptismal services, usually in our play clothes. I was fascinated with the stories of conversion I heard, and I was blessed to have many Brazilian friends whose faith formed the foundation of covenant keeping in their country. I have since realized that I had a unique perspective of how the gospel begins in small ways as the Lord builds His people and how those people and His work mature. When I was asked to speak at a Brigham Young University Emeriti luncheon on January 9, 2017, I had an opportunity to review that process and share my personal experience of seeing the gathering of the house of Israel in Brazil.

I was only four years old when we arrived in Brazil in 1958, so most of my earliest memories begin there. Those memories are full of sensory details. I remember the powerful humidity and midsummer heat, the bugs, the new critters, the vivid colors, the green foliage, the red dirt, the smells of the open markets, the ebullient and delightful people, and the bewilderment of hearing but not understanding a language I did not speak.

In no time at all, Brazil became home to us—so much so that when Daddy was released five years later, my younger brother asked, "When we go back to the Estados Unidos, will we ever come home anymore?"

THE RESTORATION OF THE GOSPEL OF JESUS CHRIST IN BRAZIL

What I didn't know as a child but have come to learn now is that I was given a front-row seat to witness the restoration of the gospel in Brazil. I have numerous ancestors who were eyewitnesses to the early Restoration of the gospel. Some of them knew Joseph Smith well, and many more assisted in the growth of the Church under the leadership of Brigham Young and other early prophets.

In every place the gospel is introduced, the Restoration begins anew. I witnessed planting of gospel seeds in Brazil. Since then, I have seen the Church grow, blossom, and bear fruit in that great country. My journey of faith began there.

In thinking about the restoration of the gospel in Brazil, I have pondered the way the Lord patiently plants seeds of faith and nourishes them until a mighty work takes place and the harvest of His precious fruit becomes a reality.

BEGINNINGS OF THE RESTORED
GOSPEL IN SOUTH AMERICA

The first effort to establish the Lord's restored Church in South America took place in 1851, when Elder Parley P. Pratt, an early Apostle, was sent to explore the possibility of beginning the Church there. During that season of early expansion, Apostles traveled to many other countries for the same purpose, fulfilling the direction of the Lord to take the gospel to all the world.[1] Elder Pratt "sailed from gold rush San Francisco to Valparaiso, Chile, along with his wife and another missionary, making the trio the first missionaries to South America. Unfortunately, civil unrest, restrictive laws against non-Catholic religions, struggles with the language, the death of an infant son, and lack of adequate funds cut short this early effort. Parley continued to study Spanish, however, and envisioned a day when the Church would sweep Latin America."[2]

Seventy-four years later, in Argentina, on the hot Christmas Day of 1925, Elder Melvin J. Ballard of the Quorum of the Twelve Apostles dedicated the continent of South America for the preaching of the gospel. At that post–World War I time, communities of European refugees were growing in South America. A few of those refugees were members of the Church. As Elder Ballard was returning home from his six-month mission in Argentina, he said: "'The work of the Lord will grow slowly for a time here just as an oak grows slowly from an acorn. It will not shoot up in a day as does the sunflower that grows quickly and then dies. But thousands will join the Church here. It will be divided into more than one mission and will be one of the strongest in the Church.'"[3]

CALLED TO THE LORD'S SERVICE

When Daddy was in his youth, he attended a stake conference in which Elder Ballard spoke about his mission to South America. My

father said that Elder Ballard's "sermons and descriptions of his journeys in South America electrified [their] community."[4] Only a few
years later, when my father was 18 years old, he received a patriarchal
blessing from his grandfather John Howard Bawden. In that blessing
he was told, "You shall travel very extensively in the ministry of the
House of Israel. . . . Yea, even in the lands of the south, 10 million of
the pure blood of Israel are waiting for that Gospel message. You will
be a power in the hands of the Lord to bring that nation to repentance,
for a nation will be born in a day."[5]

Daddy expected to serve a mission where he had English and Swiss
ancestry, but in 1939, he was called to serve in the Brazilian Mission,
a place he knew very little about. He was set apart for his mission by
Elder Melvin J. Ballard. Upon his arrival in Brazil, there were very few
members of the Church living there. Although he was assigned to
learn Portuguese, Church meetings were conducted in German. He
eventually learned to speak and read both German and Portuguese
very well. He thoroughly enjoyed serving in Brazil. For the remainder
of his life, he and his missionary companions would gather frequently
to reminisce about their service and their love for Brazil. However,
after diligently serving a three-year mission, he could not take credit
for bringing a single convert into the Church.

BRAZIL, HERE WE COME!
Peace and Confidence through Scriptures, Personal Revelation, and Prophetic Leadership

When Daddy was called to preside over the Brazilian Mission, he
was an experienced man. He had been an Air Force officer and pilot in
World War II. He had married, established a family, and started a business. He was serving as a stake president, and he had served as a bishop
and in a number of other leadership positions in the Church. He had

worked in Church welfare leadership with men like Harold B. Lee, Marion G. Romney, Thomas S. Monson, and Glen Rudd. Six years before his call to return to Brazil, he had acquired great emotional and spiritual maturity as he experienced the deaths of his first wife and one of their children. In 1958, he and his second wife, Geraldine Hamblin, were feeling fulfilled and satisfied with life, and they were enjoying their family and their new home.

After Mother and Daddy received the call to go to Brazil, they sought peace and direction as they studied scriptures in the Book of Mormon and Doctrine and Covenants concerning the gathering of Israel. They were fortified in their faith as they read that the Lamb "shall manifest himself unto all nations,"[6] that people "out of every nation under heaven" will gather to the ensign of the restored gospel,[7] and that missionaries will "call upon all nations."[8]

Before he left for Brazil, Daddy prayed earnestly, asking God two specific questions. His first question was "'Father in Heaven, do you really intend to organize and establish a strong branch of your Church and kingdom in Brazil? Are we really serious about it down there?'" He later recounted, "Before I could finish the prayer—immediately on asking the question, in fact—He answered it to me in my mind and vividly, almost with words, directed to me to turn to the Book of Mormon and read many passages that I wouldn't have been able to recall without that flash of inspiration. . . . Many passages came to my mind concerning the message to the Gentiles, and I was immediately informed by the Spirit that it didn't matter whether they belonged to the house of Israel or not. The gospel was for them."

His second question was really a request. He prayed, "'Heavenly Father, I'm willing to go on this mission, provided you'll go with me.'" Immediately, before he could finish his prayer, it seemed that the Lord said, "almost out loud, 'My boy, I'm already there.'"[9]

Armed with these pieces of personal revelation, Daddy and Mother were able to leave their home and belongings and face their new adventure with absolute faith and enthusiasm.

Over the next five years, my father would be mentored by great Church leaders who would come to learn about the peoples and cultures in South America and to monitor the work of the Church there. I remember seeing Daddy in the mission home, studying the scriptures and talking with visiting leaders. He discussed the Lord's work with President Hugh B. Brown, President Joseph Fielding Smith, and Elders Harold B. Lee, Spencer W. Kimball, and Ezra Taft Benson, who came as assigned by the First Presidency. Elder A. Theodore Tuttle of the Seventy, who oversaw the missions in South America, also came from time to time. Daddy received great strength and knowledge by counseling with these men, and throughout our time in Brazil, Mother and Daddy were continually taught and guided by the Lord, through His Holy Spirit.

Daddy's Work with the Missionaries

When we arrived in Brazil, Daddy could see that missionary work had progressed since his mission. As he began visiting the missionaries where they were working, he determined to focus their work on a number of large cities near São Paulo. Those cities were close enough that he could travel to them and return home the same day, so they were the perfect locations to begin a new era of work. Dad released some of his best and brightest missionaries from their callings as branch presidents and district leaders and said, "I want you to go to those cities, work with the Lord, and learn how He wants you to find, teach, and baptize individuals and families. When you learn how to do that, we will share what you have learned with other missionaries."

My siblings and I took turns traveling with our parents to wonderful cities with interesting names, such as Araraquara, Piracicaba, São José do Rio Preto, Rio Claro, Sorocaba, and Jundiaí. We loved playing in the beautiful parks and driving through the interesting countryside. As Daddy visited those and other branches, he shared his vision of missionaries achieving powerful faith such as was demonstrated by Peter of old—how Peter became formidable in his testimony of Jesus Christ. Daddy said, "We must pattern our actions and thoughts after the manner of our Savior, and to do this we must be directed at all times by His Spirit. Be courageous." His missionaries became fearless in their faith, enabling them to help sincere investigators cast aside objections from family members and friends, challenges with the Word of Wisdom, and other impediments to their conversion. One of his elders demonstrated this new confidence with a singular approach to meeting people. Whenever he approached a home, he announced, "*Chegamos!*"—meaning "We've arrived!" He and the other missionaries were finding the joy of working with the Lord and feeling empowered by the Holy Ghost.

Mother's Service

My mother was equally prepared to make a significant contribution to the Church in Brazil. Soon after our arrival, Daddy called her to lead the women's organizations in the mission. She recommended that her duties be shared with two other women. Those two women assumed responsibility for Primary and Young Women, and she retained the leadership of the Relief Society. She started visiting branches and teaching the sisters what it meant to be a president, a counselor, or a visiting teacher. Most of the sisters had never taught a lesson, conducted a meeting, or hosted a social event. They were learning to work with other women to accomplish a task and to serve one another.

Because Mother had been a stake missionary and a stake and ward leader, she knew how to train and prepare the leaders in the branches. She wrote a monthly letter, focusing on a different aspect of leadership or membership each month. To convey her vison for them, she closed each letter with the Portuguese word *Cresceremos,* meaning "We will grow." This one word inspired the sisters in their small groups to envision themselves in a much larger Church and see themselves as experienced members.

Mother was a registered nurse, and she had the responsibility for the health of the missionaries. She was determined that her family would be healthy, and she discovered all kinds of solutions and treatments for ailments commonly found in the tropics that were new to her. When our family arrived in Brazil, we encountered a serious outbreak of hepatitis among the missionaries. A great number of them were sick, and even more were recovering from severe illness. Those who had escaped infection were expecting to be its next victims. Because recovery from hepatitis took months, the capacity of the missionaries was greatly diminished. Mother was determined to find a way to prevent and treat that debilitating illness. Through a series of small miracles and discoveries, she learned that gamma globulin injections gave a temporary immunity to that disease. Thereafter, we all endured her very unpopular injections every three months. However, her treatment plan brought hepatitis to a halt in the mission. Because of her success, she was asked to later instruct other mission leaders in South America on how to eradicate hepatitis.[10]

Signs of Progress

Our family records indicate that in 1960, there were about 3,000 members of the Church in Brazil, and most branches had attendance of maybe 15 to 25.[11] There were no meetinghouses as we know them today. Members often met in rented buildings or in homes the Church had purchased and renovated as meetinghouses. One of my early memories is of attending a district conference in a theater. The wooden seats squeaked as they swung up and down, making it difficult for a wiggly little girl to sit still and stay quiet. During those years, a building program was established, and beautiful new buildings were constructed. One of them was in Pinheiros, São Paulo, and I was baptized there on my eighth birthday.

When we arrived in Brazil, missionaries provided most of the leadership in the branches. But my father felt that the members were ready for leadership opportunities and the personal growth that would come with responsibility. Because of the revelation he had received before departing for Brazil, he had a feeling of urgency and a personal vision of a new era of growth. His feeling was to "move, move, go, go!" He loved and had a great respect for the Brazilians. He appreciated their humility and desire to serve, and his service as a stake president had taught him that the Lord builds His Church by developing people.

Soon, Brazilians were called to most leadership positions and were making important faith-filled contributions to build the Church. As Daddy issued calls, once in a while a person would say, "I can't accept that calling. I smoke." Then Daddy would say, "You used to smoke!" As expectations changed, faith increased. Daddy met often with new leaders, helping them become ever more successful in their callings. Many, many people became great and effective leaders in those years, forming the foundation of the Church in Brazil today. When we left Brazil in 1963, we had witnessed a season of explosive growth, with approximately 14,000 members of the Church[12] preparing the way for the first stake, which would be created a few years later.[13]

THE FIRST TEMPLE IN SOUTH AMERICA
AND A FLOOD OF MISSIONARIES

Fourteen years after serving as mission president, my father, then a General Authority, was called back to Brazil to serve as the Supervisor of the Area. President Spencer W. Kimball gave him two principal assignments: to oversee the completion of the São Paulo Temple and to establish a new tradition of sending Brazilians to serve missions.

At that time, the closest temple for any member in South America was in Mesa, Arizona. A temple in São Paulo would finally make it possible for all members in South America to more easily receive the blessings of the house of Israel. It was obvious that the young people of Brazil desired this blessing, and the young women hoped to marry returned missionaries in the temple. However, very few Brazilian young men served missions. Most lived in depressed economic conditions and did not have opportunities to complete a basic education.

Under the direction of the prophet, Daddy led a plan to begin calling young Brazilians on missions. Miracles happened as young men and their leaders caught the vision of missionary service and discovered new gifts in themselves. A great and stirring vitalization occurred in the hearts of hundreds of young men. They began arriving in São Paulo ready to serve, but many of them came with little more than they could carry in a small sack. To help train this rapidly emerging missionary force, Daddy and Mother organized a three-day missionary training center, initially housing the missionaries in their garage. The missionaries walked two blocks to the stake center to shower, eat, and attend classes. The local Relief Society sisters fed them, and teachers were called to help them prepare. The trickle of missionaries soon became a stream and then an amazing surge, as they began to serve by the thousands. A new tradition of service had been born. When the São Paulo Temple was dedicated in October 1978, it seemed to be a fulfillment of Elder Melvin J. Ballard's prophecy. But this was just the beginning.

FAST FORWARD

Twenty-six years later, I returned to Brazil in the capacity of First Counselor in the Young Women General Presidency. My husband and I escorted my parents to the rededication of the São Paulo Temple. My father was then 86 years old, and though it was a difficult journey for him, he was energized to return to a people for whom he had a deep and abiding love. The vison he had received prior to his call as mission president remained clear in his memory.

When we entered the large soccer stadium where the celebration for the temple would take place, my parents were overcome with emotion. The 60,000 spectators and the 10,000 youth who were there to dance and sing were a beautiful sight. Just as the skies rained throughout the celebration, my parents wept without pause to see the spectacular presentation and enthusiasm of the Saints in Brazil.

During that visit, I was reunited with my former Primary teacher. She had served as a temple worker and as a missionary with her husband. Her posterity included at least a dozen returned missionaries. I was humbled as I recalled her as a new convert, teaching me the Articles of Faith from a small card. She did not have a manual to refer to, but she knew she could help us learn from her own testimony. She and thousands of others had devoted their lives to nurturing seeds of faith in Brazil.

As a General Officer of the Church, I visited Brazil several times. I traveled to the north and the south of the country, stopping in some cities that were not open to missionary work when I lived there. I rejoiced to meet wonderful Saints and to witness their full capacity to lead the Lord's work.

One day while waiting for a flight at an airport in northern Brazil, I met a mother and father sending their only child, a beautiful son, on his mission. After he hugged them and waved goodbye, the weeping mother asked me, "How can I do this? I just joined this Church two years ago. I don't know how to do this! This is not part of my experience. How can I say goodbye for two years?" I could not hold back my own tears as I recalled being the wiggly girl on the squeaky theater seat. My heart rejoiced as I realized I was witnessing the fulfillment of the prophecy of a great gathering into the Lord's covenant.

RESTORATION OF THE GOSPEL THROUGHOUT THE WORLD

Each Latter-day Saint has a unique perspective of the Restoration. In my lifetime, this miracle has clearly taken place in South America. When Elder Ballard dedicated that land, he prophesied that the Lord's work would begin small there, like an acorn, but that it would grow to be like an oak. I have witnessed this same growth in Brazil and throughout the world, and I have felt the power of the Prophet Joseph Smith's bold prophecy:

"The standard of truth has been erected: no unhallowed hand can stop the work from progressing. . . . The truth of God will go forth boldly, nobly, and independent till it has penetrated every continent, visited every clime, swept every country, and sounded in every ear, till the purposes of God shall be accomplished and the great Jehovah shall say the work is done."[14]

NOTES

1. See Doctrine and Covenants 107:23.
2. Matthew J. Grow, "The Extraordinary Life of Parley P. Pratt," *Ensign*, Apr. 2007, 61.

3. Melvin J. Ballard, in Bryant Hinckley, *Sermons and Missionary Services of Melvin J. Ballard* (1949), 100.

4. William Grant Bangerter, *These Things I Know: The Autobiography of William Grant Bangerter* (2013), 34.

5. Patriarchal blessing of William Grant Bangerter; in possession of the author.

6. 1 Nephi 13:42.

7. Doctrine and Covenants 64:42.

8. Doctrine and Covenants 133:8.

9. William Grant Bangerter, *These Things I Know*, 154–55.

10. See Mark L. Grover, *A Land of Promise and Prophecy: Elder A. Theodore Tuttle in South America, 1960–1965* (2008), 121–23.

11. See William Grant Bangerter, *These Things I Know*, 234.

12. See William Grant Bangerter, *These Things I Know*, 234.

13. See "Facts and Statistics: Brazil," Mormon Newsroom; available at mormonnewsroom.org/facts-and-statistics/country/brazil; accessed 17 March 2018.

14. Joseph Smith, in *Joseph Smith Papers, History, 1838–1856, volume C-1* (2 November 1838–31 July 1842)," 1285; available at josephsmith papers.org/paper-summary/history-1838-1856-volume-c-1-2-november -1838-31-july-1842/459; accessed 25 January 2018.

4

GLAD TIDINGS OF TRUTH

During my nearly 15 years of general Church service, I traveled over a million miles and met Saints in dozens of countries. I counseled with and worked closely with prophets, seers, and revelators and other General Authorities and Officers, and I saw the hand of the Lord in countless ways. Because of my service at Church headquarters, I am often asked to share highlights and lessons I learned from those special years. My participation in that monumental work helped to confirm my faith and deepen my testimony of fundamental truths. When the president of the Utah Salt Lake South Mission asked me to speak at a devotional for missionaries and friends who were learning about the Church, I took the opportunity to reflect on evidences of God's restored covenant and blessings we enjoy because the gospel has been restored.

When the Lord restored His gospel through the Prophet Joseph Smith, he opened a new era, or dispensation, of blessings for God's children.

With the Restoration of the gospel, God made the fulness of His blessings available to mankind once again. Truths that had been lost now opened our minds to new and everlasting possibilities and promises. Before the Restoration, "darkness . . . cover[ed] the earth, and gross darkness the people."[1] Now we have received "a voice of gladness! A voice of mercy from heaven; and a voice of truth out of the earth."[2]

In this dispensation of the fulness of times, the Savior and His servants "gather together in one all things in Christ, both which are in heaven, and which are on earth; even in him."[3] Because the gospel has been restored, we can learn how to become "heirs of God, and joint-heirs with Christ,"[4] "heirs of salvation."[5] We can "all come in the unity of the faith, and of the knowledge of the Son of God, . . . unto the measure of the stature of the fulness of Christ."[6] Paul's words to the Galatians can be fulfilled in us: "Ye are all one in Christ Jesus. And if ye be Christ's, then are ye Abraham's seed, and heirs according to the promise."[7]

There is much to rejoice and be glad about in the Restoration. In this brief message, I will share my witness of four evidences of that promise.

THE GATHERING OF THE HOUSE OF ISRAEL

The literal gathering of Israel is taking place throughout the world. In the Pearl of Great Price and the Old Testament, we learn of Abraham, who called himself "a follower of righteousness." We read that he "sought for the blessings of the fathers"—meaning his ancient fathers: Adam, Seth, Enoch, Noah, and others—"and the right whereunto [he] should be ordained to administer the same." He desired "to be one who possessed great knowledge, and to be a greater follower of righteousness, and to possess a greater knowledge, and to be a father of many nations, a prince of peace, and . . . to receive instructions, and to keep the commandments of God."[8]

Together, Abraham and his wife Sarah entered into a covenant with God and received the promises Abraham had sought. To Abraham, God said:

"I will make thee exceeding fruitful, and I will make nations of thee, and kings shall come out of thee.

"And I will establish my covenant between me and thee and thy seed after thee in their generations for an everlasting covenant. . . .

". . . I will bless [Sarah], and she shall be a mother of nations; kings of people shall be of her."[9]

Today we often call this the Abrahamic covenant. Abraham and Sarah and their posterity became God's covenant people. Their family chronicle is lengthy, with many side stories. The account contains prophecies and commandments and tells of people who either opted in or opted out of making covenants with God. Those who opted to keep the Lord's commandments and make covenants with Him are referred to as the house of Israel—named for Abraham and Sarah's grandson Jacob, whose name the Lord changed to Israel. They are God's covenant family.

The New Testament continues the story of that family, whose Messiah, or Anointed One, was the Lord Jesus Christ—who, as Jehovah, had established God's promises to Abraham and his faithful descendants. The Gospels of Matthew, Mark, Luke, and John record the earthly mission and ministry of the Messiah, who fulfilled the Old Testament law of Moses by offering Himself as a sacrifice for all mankind. Through His atoning sacrifice, Abraham and Sarah and their faithful descendants receive the blessings of the Abrahamic covenant. But the Savior also provides the way for all people who are not born into the bloodline of the house of Israel to opt in to the covenant, becoming equal with all His covenant family. After His death and

Resurrection, He commanded His disciples to "teach all nations,"[10] thus inviting all people to become His covenant people.

This belonging to a covenant family is what the Apostle Peter described when he told the Saints in his day that they were "a chosen generation" and "a peculiar [or distinct] people," with their own singular identity.[11] Membership in the house of Israel provides all people a heritage of faith and a future of promise.

The Book of Mormon contains many prophecies regarding the house of Israel. It teaches that this family will be gathered out of captivity into the lands of their inheritance. It teaches that the Savior will number them—or, in other words, know them personally—and that they will come to know Him.[12] The Lord's promises will be restored to them—they will have the fulness of the gospel,[13] and the Lord will remember them as part of His covenant with Abraham.[14]

In the Doctrine and Covenants, we read other prophecies about the gathering of the house of Israel. The Lord says that in the last days, "the righteous shall be gathered out from among all nations."[15]

To learn about our personal connection to God's covenant family, each baptized member of the Church can receive a patriarchal blessing, which reveals our lineage in the house of Israel.

Because the gathering of the house of Israel is so important, The Church of Jesus Christ of Latter-day Saints is serious about missionary work. We place a great deal of emphasis on preparing and sending missionaries to teach this message all over the world. Missionaries leave home and family and place their personal pursuits on pause for a season in order to serve. We have the best of training facilities in a number of nations to prepare that missionary force. Some missionaries serve close to their homes, and others travel long distances to their missions. Each has a sacred call and carries a portion of the holy apostleship as a representative of the Lord Jesus Christ.[16] It is humbling to hear their stories of enduring extreme cold or heat, culture challenges, language barriers, and encounters with danger, opposition, insects, and disease, just so they can participate in this great gathering.

In my ministry, I have visited Church members in North and South America, in Europe, in Asia, in Africa, and on the isles of the sea. In every part of the world, people are hearing the message of Jesus Christ and His doctrine. Through baptism and the gift of the Holy Ghost, they are gathering in this covenant family and seeking the blessings Abraham and Sarah sought. This identity with a spiritual ancestral family solidly connects each member to a heritage of faith and promise and provides equal blessings for all who enter that covenant.

THE BOOK OF MORMON

The Book of Mormon was written and compiled "to show unto the remnant of the house of Israel what great things the Lord hath done for their fathers; and that they may know the covenants of the Lord, that they are not cast off forever—And also to the convincing of the Jew and Gentile that JESUS is the CHRIST, the ETERNAL GOD."[17] Nephi declared the purpose of the Book of Mormon: "We talk of Christ, we rejoice in Christ, we preach of Christ, we prophesy of Christ, and we write according to our prophecies, that our children may know to what source they may look for a remission of their sins."[18]

The Book of Mormon is undeniable evidence that the heavens are not sealed and that the Lord reveals His will to His people in every age and time. Within its pages, God's covenant with His people is defined and exemplified. The book contains the continuing story of a remnant of the house of Israel on the American continent. It testifies of Jesus Christ and His preeminent leadership in God's covenant family. It tells of His interactions with His covenant people and their struggles to keep their promises to Him. It is another witness of His capacity to bless those who choose to make covenants with Him. As we read and follow the truths of the Book of Mormon, we draw nearer to Heavenly Father and Jesus Christ and Their promised blessings.

When the resurrected Christ visited His people in the Americas, He said, "I am the Lord, I change not."[19] Quoting His own words to the prophet Malachi, He spoke of those who covenant with Him: "They shall be mine, saith the Lord of Hosts, in that day when I make up my jewels; and I will spare them as a man spareth his own son that serveth him."[20]

The Book of Mormon adds to the witness of Jesus Christ established in the Bible and confirms "the promises made to the fathers."[21] It teaches that the Lord "doeth nothing save it be plain unto the children of men; and he inviteth them all to come unto him and partake of his goodness; and he denieth none that come unto him, black and white, bond and free, male and female; and he remembereth the heathen; and all are alike unto God, both Jew and Gentile."[22]

The Book of Mormon teaches that all people who repent and come unto Christ become "the covenant people of the Lord."[23] People of all backgrounds and cultures are blessed as they study this book and accept its invitation: "Seek this Jesus of whom the prophets and apostles have written, that the grace of God the Father, and also the Lord Jesus Christ, and the Holy Ghost, which beareth record of them, may be and abide in you forever."[24]

POWER THROUGH PRIESTHOOD ORDINANCES

Priesthood is an eternal power that gives us access to all the blessings of the Savior's Atonement. The priesthood connects God's covenant people to Him and to each other. It has been restored, and it is present in The Church of Jesus Christ of Latter-day Saints. It "continueth in the church of God in all generations, and is without beginning of days or end of years."[25] It is "to be used for the benefit of men, women, and children alike."[26] As Sister Elaine L. Jack taught, "When we receive the blessings of the priesthood, we are drawing on the power and grace of God."[27]

In the ordinances of the priesthood, "the power of godliness is manifest."[28] The first ordinance and covenant the Lord asks His people to receive is the ordinance of baptism, in which we are "buried with him . . . into death: that like as Christ was raised up from the dead by the glory of the Father, even so we also should walk in newness of life."[29] In this beautiful imagery, we are invited to bury our old self and arise a new person. Jesus Christ Himself showed us the example and manner of baptism. His Apostles and others called by His authority went into the world as far as they could extend their ministries. They preached: "Repent, and be baptized every one of you in the name of Jesus Christ for the remission of sins, and ye shall receive the gift of the Holy Ghost. For the promise is unto you, and to your children, and to all that are afar off, even as many as the Lord our God shall call."[30]

When we receive the ordinance of confirmation, the laying on of hands for the gift of the Holy Ghost, we receive the opportunity to be guided to all truth and to be fortified in our faith and testimony of Heavenly Father and Jesus Christ. The Holy Ghost enables powerful faith, helps us find answers to our questions, enlightens our minds, and fills our souls with joy.[31] Every time we worthily participate in the ordinance of the sacrament, we are promised the companionship of the Holy Ghost, or the Spirit. We promise to always remember the

Savior and keep His commandments, that we "may always have his Spirit to be with [us]."[32]

Later, through the ordinances we receive and the covenants we make in the temple, we are given "the key of the mysteries of the kingdom, even the key of the knowledge of God,"[33] and the potential of family relationships "forever and ever."[34] The promise to Abraham and Sarah's daughter-in-law Rebekah—to be "the mother of thousands of millions"[35]—is continued through priesthood ordinances in the temple. In holy temples, we can receive the fulness, or completeness, of the Lord's priesthood. Blessings are "poured out upon the heads of [the Lord's] people."[36] The Lord and His prophets are serious about making priesthood ordinances available to all people, living and dead. He shares His covenant with us when we receive temple ordinances, and we return to the temple to receive ordinances in behalf of ancestors who have died without that blessing.

PRIESTHOOD AUTHORITY AND KEYS

When Jesus Christ was on the earth, He authorized His disciples to use His priesthood. In Matthew chapter 10 and Luke chapters 9 and 10, we read of Him calling the Twelve Apostles, the Seventy, and others to participate in His work and perform miracles in His name. In our day, the Lord continues to authorize His servants to act in His name to bless others. This authority is shared in an orderly way through what we call keys. President Joseph F. Smith taught: "It is necessary that every act performed under [priesthood] authority shall be done at the proper time and place, in the proper way, and after the proper order. The power of directing these labors constitutes the *keys* of the Priesthood."[37]

As I have served in the Church, I have been a witness of the careful guardianship of the Lord's priesthood authority, which ensures that the Lord's covenant remains pure and available to all who desire His blessings.

Our fifth article of faith says, "We believe that a man [and, I would add, a woman] must be called of God, by prophecy, and by the laying on of hands by those who are in authority, to preach the Gospel and administer in the ordinances thereof."[38] Apostles hold all the priesthood keys necessary to lead the Lord's work on the earth, and one man directs the use of those keys. That man is always the President of the Church, the prophet. The authority to oversee the performance of ordinances and to call people to serve in the offices of the Church is disseminated through the authority given to him. Through the keys he holds, all General Authorities and General Officers act in their callings. Every stake president, bishop, mission president, and temple president receives authority to act in his office. And they, in turn, are authorized to call people in stakes and wards to fill positions of responsibility and to perform tasks that keep the Lord's work going forward.

Every person with a responsibility in The Church of Jesus Christ of Latter-day Saints serves under the authority of one who holds priesthood keys. Because of this, we all serve with authority. President M. Russell Ballard has taught, "Those who have priesthood keys . . . literally make it possible for all who serve faithfully under their direction to exercise priesthood authority and have access to priesthood power."[39] President Dallin H. Oaks added: "We are not accustomed to speaking of women having the authority of the priesthood in their Church callings, but what other authority can it be? . . . Whoever functions in an office or calling received from one who holds priesthood keys exercises priesthood authority in performing her or his assigned duties."[40]

In this Church, we do not set up camps, followings, separate authorities, or powers outside of the keys held by the prophet. We do not campaign for responsibilities, and we do not assign ourselves to fill offices. Having worked beside those who hold the responsibility for safeguarding the Lord's priesthood power, I have learned how sincerely they strive to protect the Lord's prophet and the keys he holds. I have admired the quality of restraint in this regard in all members of the First Presidency and the Quorum of the Twelve Apostles. They each carry a deep reverence for the authority delegated to them. They know that the priesthood blessings we enjoy arise from using that authority correctly.

COVENANT RESTORED

The Lord has restored His covenant to the earth. The blessings of this covenant have no qualification other than worthiness and desire to obtain them. We are witnesses of the great gathering of the house of Israel. Any person who now lives or who will live or who has ever lived on the earth will have the opportunity to be included in that covenant family. The Book of Mormon, from the first page to the last, contains powerful testimonies of Jesus Christ and His gospel. All who sincerely study its doctrines receive the blessing of knowing Him, loving Him, and becoming more like Him. The priesthood power on the earth today is for the benefit of all God's children. All who desire to be partakers of the blessings of the priesthood can enjoy them. Priesthood keys protect the Lord's covenant and ensure that every member has an equal opportunity to receive and renew essential ordinances and that all can receive the opportunity to serve under the authority of a living prophet. I am profoundly grateful for these and many other evidences that God has restored His covenant in The Church of Jesus Christ of Latter-day Saints.

NOTES

1. Isaiah 60:2.
2. Doctrine and Covenants 128:19.
3. Ephesians 1:10.
4. Romans 8:17.
5. Hebrews 1:14.
6. Ephesians 4:13.
7. Galatians 3:28–29.
8. Abraham 1:2.
9. Genesis 17:6–7, 16.
10. Matthew 28:19; see also verse 20.
11. 1 Peter 2:9.
12. See 1 Nephi 22:12, 25.
13. See 3 Nephi 16.
14. See 2 Nephi 29:13–14.
15. Doctrine and Covenants 45:71.
16. See Bible Dictionary, "Apostle," 612.
17. The title page of the Book of Mormon.
18. 2 Nephi 25:26.
19. 3 Nephi 24:6.
20. 3 Nephi 24:17; see also Malachi 3:17.
21. Doctrine and Covenants 2:2.
22. 2 Nephi 26:33.
23. 2 Nephi 30:2.
24. Ether 12:41.
25. Doctrine and Covenants 84:17.
26. Dallin H. Oaks, "The Relief Society and the Church," *Ensign*, May 1992, 36; quoted in *Daughters in My Kingdom*, 127.
27. Elaine L. Jack, "Partakers of the Glories," *Ensign*, Nov. 1996, 76; quoted in *Daughters in My Kingdom*, 127.
28. Doctrine and Covenants 84:20; see also verses 19, 21–22.
29. Romans 6:4.
30. Acts 2:38–39.
31. See Doctrine and Covenants 11:13–14.
32. Doctrine and Covenants 20:77.
33. Doctrine and Covenants 84:19.
34. Doctrine and Covenants 132:19.

35. Genesis 24:60.

36. Doctrine and Covenants 110:10.

37. Joseph F. Smith, in *Teachings of Presidents of the Church: Joseph F. Smith* (1998), 224.

38. Articles of Faith 1:5.

39. M. Russell Ballard, "Men and Women in the Work of the Lord," *New Era,* Apr. 2014, 4.

40. Dallin H. Oaks, "The Keys and Authority of the Priesthood," *Ensign,* May 2014, 51.

5

AN AMAZING GIFT

One of the most inspiring, challenging, fulfilling, and stretching experiences of my life was the assignment to direct the preparation of a written history of Relief Society for the worldwide Church. Until the book was completed, I carried that responsibility constantly in my heart, and my mind was often consumed by thoughts and feelings about the project. I prayed for endurance as I worked many times through the night, and I hoped I would not ruin my eyes as I reviewed page layouts and text on the small screen of my phone in far-flung places of the world. The result of that prophetic assignment was the publication of Daughters in My Kingdom: The History and Work of Relief Society *in 2011. The history came at a time when the women of the Church needed to know of their value, not just as spirit children of heavenly parents but as indispensable, integral, and essential contributors to the building of the Lord's kingdom on the earth. In March 2016, I was asked to speak at the Church History Symposium to commemorate the fifth anniversary of the publication of that history and to share the inspiration and story behind its creation.*

THE NEED FOR *DAUGHTERS IN MY KINGDOM*
Instructions from Living Prophets

When Silvia H. Allred, Barbara Thompson, and I were called to serve as the Relief Society General Presidency, we were given very clear instructions. President Gordon B. Hinckley asked me pointedly to help him not only take care of Relief Society but to help the women of the Church become more committed to the restored gospel of Jesus Christ. He expressed a deep concern about all Relief Society sisters but especially those who were not fully converted to the gospel and who were searching for identity and purpose. He also expressed a concern for the young women who were moving into Relief Society. He wanted them to know the importance of the organization they were entering and the work they would be enlisted in for the remainder of their lives. He was very clear and firm with me about the authority I would have as Relief Society General President. After we were sustained in general conference, I was set apart to "preside over the great worldwide sisterhood" of Relief Society.[1]

From the beginning of our assignment, the First Presidency and the Quorum of the Twelve Apostles invited us to be partners with them at a time of inflection, or a "hastening," of the work of salvation. We were given insight into how they saw the Church moving forward, and we received a confirmation of their charge to take the gospel to all the world. In our visits with them, we were touched by their sincere concern for the women of the Church and their feelings of urgency about moving the Lord's work forward. When I asked if Relief Society had a significant role to play in that work, I received a strong, affirmative answer. We were told: "We can't do it without you. Speak the truth. We are past pleasantries—we must measure up."[2]

MYTHS ABOUT THE WOMEN OF THE CHURCH AND RELIEF SOCIETY

It was not long before we confronted prominent and damaging myths regarding the women of the Church and Relief Society. Many women and men inside and outside the Church had adopted the notions that most of the interesting stories in Church history were about men, that women were second-class citizens in the Church, that Latter-day Saint women were generally sweet but largely uninformed, and that Relief Society itself was in its waning season, having no real function or standing in modern times beyond a Sunday classroom experience. And sadly, we also discovered that many Latter-day Saint women felt they would never be good enough, intelligent enough, talented enough, or prominent enough to be equal partners with men in the Church and at home.

As Church leaders strove to fulfill their mandate to "bring [the Church] forth out of obscurity,"[3] it was obvious that if the women of the Church felt obscure or were seen as obscure, then a large and essential segment of the Church population would not be fully engaged in hastening the Lord's work.

In the midst of an explosion of information and technology, we discovered that for many—if not most—of our sisters, there was confusion about our purpose and work. We could see that many local congregations had developed personal traditions and adaptations to Relief Society that, though they were often sincere, were inconsistent with the purpose of the organization. As the Church had grown to span the globe, there seemed to be confusion about the identity of Latter-day Saint women and the purpose of Relief Society. Like other general Relief Society leaders before us, we realized that our identity and purpose were not being communicated effectively across the diversity of languages, cultures, economies, and experiences in the Church.

We needed a way to transmit the true spirit and contribution of Latter-day Saint women, a way to communicate our purpose and achieve global alignment.

LEARNING ABOUT FEMALE DISCIPLES IN THE LORD'S WORK

In order to approach the challenges we were encountering and fulfill the mandate that had been given us, we went to the Lord for direction as to what we needed to know and do. We knew we needed to learn more.

Our first challenge was to fully determine the scope of our own work. In essence, we went "to school." As a presidency, we began to study the scriptures to look for any special patterns, instructions, and "breadcrumbs" that could lead the way to what we were organized to do. We pondered the Lord's work "to bring to pass the immortality and eternal life of man."[4] We studied what we could do to assist His prophets and apostles in the Church's purpose "that faith . . . might increase in the earth; that [the Lord's] everlasting covenant might be established; that the fulness of [His] gospel might be proclaimed by the weak and the simple unto the ends of the world, and before kings and rulers."[5] Our study of the scriptures revealed the vast scope of global work that needed to be accomplished.

We found in the scriptures that the Savior Jesus Christ had a pattern of calling and organizing male and female disciples to assist Him in His work.[6] We read of women and men worshipping together in sacred settings.[7] We read that the Lord would pour out His Spirit upon sons and daughters and upon servants and handmaids.[8] We read of sisters having "business" to take care of as "helpers in Christ Jesus"[9] and being yoked with male disciples as "fellowlabourers"[10] in the Lord's ancient Church. We studied Church history and the work of previous Relief Society General Presidents. These and other learnings confirmed our belief that God expected and planned for a full commitment from His daughters as well as His sons in His work.

We also studied several academic works that taught us about global communication and how organizations find their purpose and meaning among the plethora of messages filling the world today. It was interesting to learn about "brands" and how companies and organizations achieve lasting success. We wanted to know what makes a brand thrive and endure across cultures and languages. We learned that if Relief Society was a brand or a product, fewer and fewer people were buying it. In our study, we discovered that lasting brands depended on the ability to deliver a genuine and credible story that could convey an organization's underlying purpose. It became clear to us that without a compelling story, we would find it difficult to resonate with women and men on a global scale. We could see a clear correlation between men and women of the Church not knowing about or believing in our "brand" and the probable disenfranchisement that could reflect upon every sister in Relief Society.

At one point we were given some research indicating that individuals who know and understand Church history are much more likely to be faithful in their spiritual observance and to have a greater sense of identity in the Church. That discovery made much more sense in light of the fact that a record of spiritual lineage was vitally important to the families in the Book of Mormon. We read over and over again in the Book of Mormon about the responsibility of leaders to keep a record of their "story." We saw the significance of that kind of historical connection for Relief Society.

We studied as much Relief Society history as we could find, and then we studied it again. We were given access to a great deal of information provided by Church historians and senior Church leaders. We also had access to senior Church leaders themselves. Our dear President Boyd K. Packer had compiled a treasured and extensive private archive of Relief Society history. He gave that history to us and was also generous with his time, repeatedly sharing his spiritual witness and insights about the meaning of Relief Society in the Lord's Church and kingdom.

DISTILLING THE PURPOSE OF RELIEF SOCIETY

After a season of study, we went to the First Presidency to ask if we were developing the right focus. We told them that we believed we had distilled the purpose of Relief Society. We presented to them a paper that said, "Relief Society was organized to help sisters prepare for the blessings of eternal life as they increased faith and personal righteousness, strengthened families and homes and provided relief to those in need."

The answer from the First Presidency was a resounding "YES!" We were told, "Carry on with that!"

So, we now had delineated our purpose, and it had received approval. To move us forward in a global age, the purpose of Relief Society could now be stated in three words: *Faith, Family,* and *Relief.* This purpose was simple and clear enough to be understood and applied across cultures and languages. Our study of history had revealed a distinct purpose that had carried the women of the Church through changing world conditions—through wars, pestilences, natural disasters, famines, and global expansion.

Now that we were able to articulate a clear, straightforward purpose, we hoped to find a way to share the compelling story behind it.

We began talking about the need to give sisters the tools and skills to carry out their purpose in their own lives. We recalled that the second Relief Society General President, Sister Eliza R. Snow, carefully preserved the minutes of the first Relief Society meetings containing instructions from the Prophet Joseph Smith, which he said were meant to be the "constitution and law" for the sisters.[11] Sister Snow used that minute book for many years as she traveled and taught Relief Society and priesthood leaders to firmly establish their work. Since our work had now spread around the world and since so many sisters were striving to keep their covenants in relative isolation, I asked myself and others if it would be useful for every sister to have something that would function as her personal "minute book." In order to achieve global alignment, would it be important for each sister to have a "constitution," or a "blueprint," to follow? Was there a way to tell the captivating story of Relief Society, to solidify the identity of Latter-day Saint women and engage the sisters in the work of salvation?

THE PROCESS OF CREATING
DAUGHTERS IN MY KINGDOM

Then came the day when we received a momentous assignment from the First Presidency and the Quorum of the Twelve Apostles: to compile an official history of Relief Society for the worldwide Church audience.[12] Knowing that seers can see things others cannot see, we knew that this opportunity was not a casual assignment. We sensed that such a record had been envisioned for a long time and that now was the time to bring forth the true narrative of Latter-day Saint women. In our discussions, we sensed that this was not to be a historian's history, a biography, a chronology, or a comprehensive history. It was envisioned as a record that would convey a spiritual legacy. It was to be the vehicle to carry our purpose into homes and hearts worldwide, to be understood and applied across cultures, languages, economies, and experiences.

Assembling a Team

We were instructed that this project was to be directed by the Relief Society General Presidency, not by a curriculum department or a team of writers, and that we had "the full backing of the First Presidency and the Quorum of the Twelve Apostles" in our assignment.[13] We were told to keep the project out of the normal machinery of publication. "You are the presidency," we were told. "You are the ones who should decide what it looks like and what it feels like and how it's going to be used. We're not going to tell you what it is; you're going to tell us what it is, you're going to bring it to us when it's finished."[14]

After pondering the assignment as a presidency, we made a recommendation, and under the authority of prophets, seers, and revelators, Susan Winder Tanner was called to be the compiler and writer of the history. Susan is a woman with a full understanding of Relief Society and the personal qualities of humility and gifted intellect, and she is a woman who knows how to access the powers of heaven. She believes in and expects miracles. Church leaders gave her the charge that the book needed to "get the women of the world and the women of the Church from where they are to where they need to be."[15]

We gave Susan the large stack of reading material that we had studied and asked her to study it. We asked her to get a feeling for the spirit of the work—not to write for a while but to return when she felt she had some idea about the content of the book.

She asked if we had already developed an outline or table of contents. I replied that yes, we had a good sense of what it should look like but that we would give her time to read and assimilate the information she had and see if an outline suggested itself to her as she studied. After about three months, she called and said she was ready to share some impressions about content. I remember with joy the moment she laid her proposed outline on the table. I then placed next to it the table of contents that had been revealed to our presidency months previously. The two outlines matched. We sat for a few moments, observing the tender, thrilling significance that we were being taught from on high. We knew that we could now thrust forward with confidence in His power, being assured that He would give us what we needed—and *who* we needed—to accomplish His work.

We had been instructed not to let the editor ruin it. So after sincere prayer, we requested the assistance of Aaron West, who came to the project with the rare ability to be skeptical, as all good editors must be, and the requisite humility and willingness to be taught by the Spirit. His ability to sense the truth of what Susan was writing and continue with her consistent voice was a tremendous blessing. As we contemplated the design of the book, we had some distinct impressions about how the book should look and feel. It needed to be feminine but suggest strength. The colors must have no cultural overtones, and the design should have a global appeal. We sensed that the book needed to have a timeless, historical quality. We knew that it needed to be very visual and that the pictures and illustrations should teach as powerfully as the words. We knew that although we lived in an era when most women were able to read, many did not have a tradition or habit of reading, so the book needed to be organized into small, reader-friendly learning boosts to reach nonreaders as well as the well-read. And the book needed to fit comfortably with the slightly larger size of international scriptures for ease of carrying on buses and on long walks to meetings. As we thought about the size of the book, we hoped that it would easily fall open on a woman's lap or on a table. With those few instructions and after careful review of several ideas, a design submitted by Nicole Erickson Walkenhorst was selected.

Under the direction of Tadd Peterson, Nicole led an inspired design team, creating a beautiful book that draws the reader into every page.

Each new member of the production team felt almost immediately that this project was being directed from heaven, and they began to feel the Spirit of the Lord in their individual and collaborative efforts.

In addition to these helpers, I personally felt the interest, the love, the strength, and the power of the women who had played parts in leading and serving in Relief Society in the past.

A Miraculous Process

A continuous string of miracles and heavenly interventions became part of this seminal creative experience. Coupled with the profound blessings we were feeling was an almost constant opposition, which is well known to others who have experience working on projects such as this. Occasionally during the process, someone would become worried about not working fast enough or coming up against a roadblock that might derail the project, but our feeling was to push forward each day, be at peace, and keep moving. The Spirit said, "Move it, move it, move it," without pause.

Miraculously, a little less than a year from the day we established the outline, we pushed the start button at the printing press. Anyone with knowledge of book publishing will tell you that is an unheard-of timeline in which to research, write, design, edit, review, and print a work of this scope.

Once the printing press started, it ran almost continuously for two months to produce the initial English copies. All the while, the book was being translated into 25 languages, including English Braille. It was sent in the fall of 2011 to Relief Society sisters worldwide at no personal cost to them. The book also went online in multiple languages, with its own website, at the same time it was released in English.

WHAT *DAUGHTERS IN MY KINGDOM* TEACHES US

Daughters in My Kingdom has become a gift to those who have received it. I have pondered what members have found as they have "unwrapped" the gift. How has it illuminated our purpose and helped us with our needs? Quoting from the book itself, I review samples of what we learn:

- We learn that Relief Society was a restoration of an ancient pattern. It "belongs to the organization of the Church of Christ, in all dispensations" (Eliza R. Snow).[16] "Its organization was a necessary step in the unfolding of God's work on the earth."[17]

- We learn that with the official organization of Relief Society came "a wide and extensive sphere of action and usefulness" (Eliza R. Snow).[18] Sisters are told that by seeking to perform every duty, "you will find that your capacity will increase, and you will be astonished at what you can accomplish" (Eliza R. Snow).[19]

- We learn that faithful sisters have access to the blessings, authority, and power of the priesthood[20]—that through those blessings, "the power of godliness will be manifest to [them]" (Ezra Taft Benson).[21]

- We learn that "it is within the privilege of the sisters of this Church to receive exaltation in the kingdom of God and receive authority and power as queens and priestesses" (Joseph Fielding Smith).[22]

- We learn that Relief Society as an organization and the sisters as individual members of that organization have a parallel work with priesthood quorums. This "great sisterhood of service" (Amy Brown Lyman)[23] was organized to carry out the work of salvation[24] and to help bishops manage the Lord's storehouse of talents and resources.[25]

• We learn that "there is a great need to rally the women of the Church to stand with and for the Brethren in stemming the tide of evil that surrounds us and in moving forward the work of our Savior" (Howard W. Hunter).[26]

• We learn of Relief Society sisters' responsibility to become spiritually and temporally self-reliant and to become "sister scriptorians" (Spencer W. Kimball).[27]

• We learn that righteous women are "the guardians of the hearth" and that "no other work reaches so close to divinity as does the nurturing of the sons and daughters of God" (Gordon B. Hinckley);[28] that Relief Society sisters can "be strengthened for the challenges of the day," that they can "be endowed with wisdom beyond [their] own in dealing with the problems [they] constantly face," and that their "prayers and [their] pleadings [will] be answered with blessings upon [their] heads and upon the heads of [their] loved ones" (Gordon B. Hinckley).[29]

• We learn that through Relief Society, "the Prophet Joseph Smith turned the key for the emancipation of womankind" (George Albert Smith).[30]

• We learn that "this great circle of sisters . . . might be likened to a refuge [and a] sanctuary . . . [that] encircles each sister like a protecting wall" (Boyd K. Packer).[31]

• We learn that Latter-day Saint women are to "lead the world and to lead especially the women of the world, in everything that is praise-worthy." They "are called by the voice of the Prophet of God to do it, to be uppermost, to be the greatest and the best" (Joseph F. Smith).[32]

Daughters in My Kingdom has filled me with gratitude for the examples and testimonies of strong, capable, influential women who knew that through the ordinances of the gospel, they had the gifts and power necessary to triumph over life's challenges and to help others do the same. I am blessed by knowing that they spoke to God and understood when He spoke to them.

DAUGHTERS IN MY KINGDOM: A BLUEPRINT FOR COVENANT KEEPING

I have been asked if *Daughters in My Kingdom* is making a difference. Has it been able to meet the needs that it was envisioned to address? Is anyone reading it or using it? Does it align women behind a clear purpose and a genuine story?

My first observation of the book's impact on others occurred at the printing press on the day the first signatures emerged from the press. A woman who was checking the quality of the printed pages was reading them as fast as she could. With obvious excitement, she said there was a spirit in those pages and that she had never known those things before.

During my tenure as president, the general Relief Society office received many notes expressing gratitude for the book, and we often heard of sisters, wards, and stakes using it to teach various principles. We also heard from bishops and stake presidents who used the book to help men and young men who had pornography addictions. After these men and young men read the book, they would often return to their priesthood leaders and say, "Now I know what a real woman is like."

In my family, we use the book as a bridge to help our granddaughters move from young womanhood to adult service and leadership in the Church. We use the book, including its examples of faithful women, to teach them of their identity and purpose. We use the book to teach our grandsons and granddaughters about the priesthood. We use it to teach principles of self-reliance and watchcare. We see the book as a "constitution," or a "blueprint," for our family and our Church service.

A few years ago, I met a young woman from a small and obscure village in China. As I recall, she had grown up herding goats, and her parents, desiring that she receive a better education, had sacrificed to send her to Australia to attend high school. While in Australia, she had been contacted by missionaries and had joined the Church. She had served a mission and was just completing her degree at BYU–Hawaii. After a number of years away from home, she was now at the point of going back to China. She was worried about what would happen to her, what her future would hold. My concern for her future was tempered by my understanding that she had her own testimony and conversion to the gospel of Jesus Christ, she had her scriptures, and she would have a copy of *Daughters in My Kingdom*. Just as Sister Eliza Snow carried her minute book, this young woman would have her own "constitution" to take with her. Wherever her life experience took her, she would know how to live the Relief Society purpose of faith, family, and relief, remaining aligned with a global sisterhood in that purpose.

PART OF THE LORD'S HASTENING WORK

Creating *Daughters in My Kingdom* was a spiritual journey for me, and it became a record of a spiritual legacy.

In the Book of Mormon, we learn of Alma entrusting Helaman with the records of the people and testifying of the value of those records. Alma tells Helaman that the records "should be kept and handed down from one generation to another" and that though it might appear to be foolishness, "by small and simple things are great things brought to pass" and that sacred records "are preserved for a wise purpose, which purpose is known unto God."[33] *Daughters in My Kingdom* is not scripture, but it is a marvelous spiritual record, prepared and preserved for a wise purpose.

In 1976, President Spencer W. Kimball said, "There is a power in this organization [of Relief Society] that has not yet been fully exercised to strengthen the homes of Zion and build the Kingdom of God—nor will it be until both the sisters and the priesthood catch the vision of Relief Society."[34]

Daughters in My Kingdom teaches our identity, our purpose, and our sacred responsibility to assist the Lord with His work of salvation. It defines a spiritual legacy and invites women to "live up to [their] privilege" so they can have angels as their associates.[35] I treasure the memory of the Spirit pervading our lives as we worked on the book. I hope I never forget the wonder of it and the love that is in it.

NOTES

1. Setting apart blessing of Julie B. Beck; in possession of the author.
2. Julie B. Beck journal.
3. Doctrine and Covenants 1:30.
4. Moses 1:39.
5. Doctrine and Covenants 1:21–23.
6. See Luke 10; Doctrine and Covenants 20; 25.
7. See Acts 1:13–14.
8. See Joel 2:28–29; Acts 2:17–18.
9. See Romans 16:1–4.
10. Philippians 4:3.
11. Joseph Smith, in Relief Society Minute Book, Nauvoo, Illinois, Mar. 17, 1842, 8; available at josephsmithpapers.org/paper-summary/minutes -17-march-1842/3; accessed 17 April 2018; quoted in *Daughters in My Kingdom: The History and Work of Relief Society* (2011), 16.

12. I have spoken with some of the people who were most instrumental in bringing the book forth, and I hope to represent them and their feelings about it. However, any student of history knows that each of us recalls similar events differently. These recollections are my own. I have tried to be true to how I recorded experiences in journals and working notes, confirming those with other accounts.

13. Julie B. Beck journal.

14. Julie B. Beck journal.

15. Susan W. Tanner, "23: Sister Tanner's Writing Experience—*Daughters in My Kingdom*," Mormon Channel; available at https://www.mix cloud.com/reliefsociety/23-sister-tanners-writing-experience-daughters -in-my-kingdom/; accessed 17 April 2018.

16. In Relief Society Minutes, Third Ward, Salt Lake Stake, Sept. 23, 1868, Church History Library, 17; quoted in *Daughters in My Kingdom : The History and Work of Relief Society* (2011), 43.

17. *Daughters in My Kingdom* (2011), 16.

18. "Female Relief Society," *Deseret News*, Apr. 22, 1868, 81; quoted in *Daughters in My Kingdom* (2011), 44.

19. "An Address by Miss Eliza R. Snow," *Millennial Star*, Jan. 13, 1874, 21; quoted in *Daughters in My Kingdom* (2011), 59.

20. See *Daughters in My Kingdom* (2011), chapter 8.

21. "What I Hope You Will Teach Your Children about the Temple," *Ensign*, Aug. 1985, 10; quoted in *Daughters in My Kingdom* (2011), 129.

22. "Relief Society—an Aid to the Priesthood," *Relief Society Magazine*, Jan. 1959, 5–6; quoted in *Daughters in My Kingdom* (2011), 133.

23. *In Retrospect* (1945), 160–61; quoted in *Daughters in My Kingdom* (2011), 79.

24. See *Daughters in My Kingdom* (2011), 7, 138.

25. See *Daughters in My Kingdom* (2011), 41.

26. "To the Women of the Church," *Ensign*, Nov. 1992, 96; quoted in *Daughters in My Kingdom* (2011), 157.

27. "The Role of Righteous Women," *Ensign*, Nov. 1979, 102; quoted in *Daughters in My Kingdom* (2011), 50.

28. "Stand Strong against the Wiles of the World," *Ensign*, Nov. 1995, 101; quoted in *Daughters in My Kingdom* (2011), 148–49.

29. "Stand Strong against the Wiles of the World," *Ensign*, Nov. 1995, 101; quoted in *Daughters in My Kingdom* (2011), 165.

30. "Address to Members of Relief Society," *Relief Society Magazine*, Dec. 1945, 717; quoted in *Daughters in My Kingdom* (2011), 87.

31. "The Circle of Sisters," *Ensign*, Nov. 1980, 110; quoted in *Daughters in My Kingdom* (2011), 86.

32. In Minutes of the General Board of Relief Society, Mar. 17, 1914, Church History Library, 54–55; quoted in *Daughters in My Kingdom* (2011), 179–80.

33. Alma 37:4, 6, 8, 12.

34. Spencer W. Kimball, "Relief Society—Its Promises and Potential," *Ensign*, Mar. 1976, 4; quoted in *Daughters in My Kingdom* (2011), 142.

35. See Joseph Smith, in Relief Society Minute Book, Nauvoo, Illinois, Apr. 28, 1842, 38–39; available at josephsmithpapers.org/paper-summary /discourse-28-april-1842-as-reported-by-eliza-r-snow/4; accessed 17 April 2018; quoted in *Daughters in My Kingdom*, 181.

Purpose

"Go to, and call servants, that we may labor diligently with our might in the vineyard, that we may prepare the way, that I may bring forth again the natural fruit, which natural fruit is good and the most precious above all other fruit."

—Jacob 5:61

6

LEARNING FROM EXPERIENCE

Lessons from Blinker Lights, Spare Change, and Bologna Sandwiches

What an experience! This is how I describe my personal journey through higher education. When the dean of students at Brigham Young University asked me to address the College of Family, Home, and Social Sciences in October 2014, he wanted me to share memories of activities and friendships while attending the university. I suspect that the following message was not what he anticipated. I invited my mother, siblings, husband, and children to the speech because my experience included all of them. We shared laughter and a few tears as I recalled lessons from my years of working to earn a university degree and how those lessons have helped me strive harder to keep my covenants.

When we begin to understand who we are, we also begin to desire to know why we are here. Life is a school, and we cannot live a day without being confronted with choices or situations or people who impact the course and direction of our lives. There is so much of life we do not control. But we can learn from our experiences, and the lessons we learn can add to a firm foundation that will help us understand our purpose and make righteous choices.

In my ministry as Relief Society General President, I often conducted question-and-answer sessions with Latter-day Saint women. Many sisters' comments revealed that their life experiences were not what they felt they should be and that their good desires often did not come to fruition. For instance, someone would say, in essence, "I wish I had a husband," and then somebody else would say, in essence, "I wish I had a *different* husband." Someone would say, "I wish I had children," and then someone else would say that she wanted her children to be different or make different choices. Some wrestled with financial challenges. Others grappled with poor health or with the poor health of family members. Most had struggles that required greater faith and determination than they had anticipated. It was obvious that most were not living the dream they had hoped for.

As I pondered these discussions, I realized that we sometimes desire to live a dream life now, forgetting that earth life is about having an experience that prepares us for the promised dream of eternal life.

People have asked questions about our mortal experience throughout time, all the way back to Adam and Eve. We could say that Adam and Eve started out with an opportunity, not knowing how their experience would turn out. The book of Moses records their reflections on some of the things they learned. Adam said that because of his transgression—or, as I like to think of it, because of his mortal experience—his eyes were opened. He learned to have joy, and he understood that he would see God again in the flesh.[1] Then Eve added that because of their transgression—or in other words, because of their mortal experience—they were able to have children. (Wouldn't you like to read the volumes Eve could have written about her experiences as a mother?) She also said that because of their experience, she and Adam had learned the difference between good and evil and had come to know the joy of their redemption and eternal life, which was promised to all the obedient.[2] These were significant life lessons that came as a result of their mortal experience.

As I think about our mortal experience, I am reminded of lessons I have learned from my days as a college and university student. Although this may seem to be a message about higher education, and perhaps it is, the bigger message I hope to convey is that as we set goals and take steps into the future, we almost always have a different experience from what we imagined at the outset. But the Lord is giving us opportunities to learn and grow, and often those experiences are exactly what we need. Because the experience of higher education is usually bound by a beginning and an end, I have looked back on lessons I learned during that season as a microcosm of life and the larger life experience we all are given.

A FAMILY GOAL

My higher education experience began before I was born. When Mother and Father were on their honeymoon, they started to make some goals for their family. Both of them were the first university graduates in their families, and they wanted all their children to graduate from a university.

When they agreed on a family goal of higher education, my father said, "I'm not a wealthy man. We cannot plan on paying for higher education for our children." So mom wrote *WORK* under the goal. They would teach their children to work so they could achieve that goal. What they didn't know was that their family would grow to include 10 children. And yet, as the number of children increased, that goal never changed. When they passed that dream to their children, they didn't know they would be involved in helping their children with higher education for 25 years. They didn't know all the sacrifices their children would make to succeed in the classroom or all the ways their children would have to work to earn money for that education.

Eventually, all 10 of us graduated from Brigham Young University. Each one of my siblings could tell their own story about work—the difficulties they encountered and the lessons they learned along the way to that family goal. In telling my story, I honor each of them. They were my examples and support.

From the time I was very young, my years in formal education did not go smoothly. I often had poor health as a child, which meant I got behind in school, which meant I was always trying to catch up to my peers and improve my learning skills. When it came time to take college entrance exams, I didn't score as well as I had hoped. My high school counselor took me aside and told me to avoid going to college. She told me that I would not do well in a higher education environment and that I should do something else. But because of our family goal, I didn't know what else to do, and I stubbornly thought, "I don't care what you say. I'm going to go to college!"

DIXIE COLLEGE

My parents encouraged some of us to begin our higher education experience at smaller schools, and I began to explore my options. I had visited my sister Glenda at Ricks College in Rexburg, Idaho, long enough to know that the weather in Idaho was too cold for me. At that time, my parents had connections in southern Utah, and my father decided to buy a mobile home in the middle of a retirement community in St. George for my cousins and me to live in so we could attend Dixie College there.

When it came time to go to school, I didn't have quite enough money saved. Glenda was preparing to serve a mission, and she said that if I made her dresses, I could have what was left in her savings after she left. She got a suitcase full of dresses, and I went off to Dixie.

The day my mother and my aunt drove my cousin Robyn and me to St. George stands out in my memory. Robyn and I were so excited to be on our own and experience life away from our parents. After our mothers helped us move into the trailer, they drove off in our gold station wagon, leaving us standing on the hillside above St. George. The moment was quiet, and a dry, hot breeze ruffled our hair as we watched the blinker at the bottom of the hill go *flash, flash, flash.* Then the traffic light changed, the car turned left, and we were on our own in St. George. Jubilation lasted for about 30 seconds, and then we stared at each other and simultaneously said, "What are we going to do now?" We didn't have directions to campus, and we didn't know our way around the city, and we didn't have a car. The next day, other friends moved in, and somehow we made our way to campus, got ourselves registered for school, and were on our way.

I had a great experience at Dixie. I was stretched in many ways, and it was a season of tremendous growth. What I didn't realize at that time, but have reflected on since, is that all the students were there on new and semi-equal footing. We were making a fresh start in life, and we were willing to participate in activities we had thought we were not popular enough, courageous enough, or skilled enough to take part in during high school.

I had viewed myself as a shy person, and I consciously thought, "No one here knows I am shy, so I can pretend I'm not shy, and then I may make more friends." I determined to expand my sphere, so I tried out for the drill team and made it. I sang with Program Bureau, a performing group, and was even asked to solo a couple of times. I became involved in student leadership. I taught Gospel Doctrine in Sunday School. I played tennis. I went for hikes and walks in that beautiful red rock country. I made friends from other states and backgrounds. I tried to engage in all the best aspects of college life. I had a job on campus. I struggled in some classes and succeeded in others.

I was on my own, so I had to learn to interact with adults as never before and to advocate for myself and to seek help when I needed it. I had a number of professors and administrators whom I still remember with great fondness because of the personal interest they took in the students. I learned much from them personally and admired their ability to lift developing students, encouraging them to taste success, sometimes for the first time in their lives. I learned more about relationships by having roommates. We laughed a lot and cried rarely. I discovered Zion National Park, the Virgin River, Silver Reef, Pine Valley, Snow Canyon, and other places of spectacular beauty. I learned to love my family more and to treasure the upbringing I had been given. Almost every experience I had at Dixie was new for me, and overall, it was a wonderful season of learning.

The summer after my freshman year, I met Ramon Beck in a young single adult Sunday School class. At the end of a year and a half at Dixie, I completed my associate degree, went home, and got married.

BRIGHAM YOUNG UNIVERSITY

The day Ramon and I were married, we drove from the temple in Salt Lake City to Provo and paid our tuition at Brigham Young University. My experience at BYU was entirely different from my time at Dixie. I didn't make new lifelong friends there. As a commuter, I never lived on or near the campus. I did not participate in any extracurricular activity.

After we paid our tuition, we had three dollars left and a month to wait until the next payday. We lived with Grandpa Strong, who needed someone in his home with him at night. In return for our lodging, I cooked some of his meals and cleaned his house, and Ramon helped him get dressed and care for himself and provided stability in his increasing confusion. As we drove our old Plymouth back and forth to Provo, almost daily we experienced our own "cruse of oil" that would not fail.[3] Every time we needed gas for our car, we checked our pockets. We always found just enough change to put gas in the car and drive to school. I realized years later that change has to come from somewhere, and we never had a dollar to make change with. Somehow, the Lord provided for us to continue driving to school— never an abundance, but enough.

Both of us found employment and went to school full time. I remember that first semester as a long, cold winter, with hours studying and coming home late at night. I also remember sweet times: meeting for lunch on campus, taking care of Grandpa, learning and managing new roles.

After the first semester, we simply did not have enough money for both of us to continue in school, so I took a break and kept working to help my husband finish his education. We moved forward with our lives. Ramon graduated, and we rejoiced to welcome two children to our family. We served in our family, in the Church, and in our community. We were happy and busy with many obligations.

After a few years, the pressure to finish school began to weigh on me. The family goal was still in my heart. My younger siblings had started going to BYU, and some of them were graduating. I still needed to do my part to fulfill the family dream. Again, Glenda stepped in to help. She said, "I know you want to finish your university education. I will watch your children if you will go back to school."

Because of the time lapse since my education at Dixie College and because of policy changes at BYU, many of my credits from Dixie were not transferable. It was disheartening to learn that returning to school was almost a fresh beginning. I sat down with an advisor and asked, "What is the fastest way out of here?" He gave me some options for degrees that could be completed as quickly as possible. I chose child development and family relationships because it fit in with my career at the time, which was being a wife and a mother.

Ramon and I determined that I would attend class three days a week. I always took a full load of 18 hours because then I would receive the most credit hours for my tuition. We didn't have money to waste, and I had to finish school in the shortest amount of time. On Monday, Wednesday, and Friday, I would leave home when my family was still in bed and return home at night when they were asleep again. But on the other days, I didn't take books out of the closet or do homework. I had many other responsibilities to attend to.

Ramon was often serving with the young men in our ward, and he was also filling assignments in the Utah Army National Guard, which meant he was away from home a lot of weekends. For all that time as a student at BYU, I was in my ward Primary presidency, and for five of those years I was Primary president. During those five years, our ward was divided four times, which involved organizing and training new teachers and leaders. It was my responsibility to keep the older Primary boys moving ahead with their Scouting and to work with members of the bishopric and the ward council.

We established a pattern: I attended school for a semester, and then I paused for a semester so we could catch our breath and save more money for tuition. When I was not a full-time student, I worked on an independent study class or two, trying to chip away at my graduation requirements. I handwrote all my assignments in the library, and Ramon typed every one, without the aid of a personal computer.

When I was in school, I usually stopped by my parents' home in the morning to see which younger siblings were going to ride with me that day. My siblings and I had our own small corner of the library where we studied together. We ate the bologna sandwiches Mother had made for us. She made identical lunches for everyone, and I was always included. (By the way, I have to make a personal admission here. I strongly dislike bologna. But I didn't want to give Mother extra work, and I appreciated her thoughtfulness, so I ate her sandwiches every day I was on campus. I was always grateful for them, but I have not eaten bologna since my graduation from BYU.) My siblings and I helped each other study for exams and complete assignments. Sometimes we even filled in for one another by attending one another's classes and taking notes.

I actually enjoyed going back to campus as an older student. As a mother and a wife and a Primary president, I now knew what a priority was. I learned differently from when I was a young, single student. I prioritized my study time better. I had a more clear and active mind. I had energy, enthusiasm, and respect for the learning process. My time away from my family was a sacrifice, so the opportunity to learn was more precious than it had been before.

I was happy to discover that I could compete quite well academically. For the first time in my life, I was successful in school, and I loved that feeling. In the years I had been away from academia, I had acquired better skills in memorizing and learning. I knew how to apply myself better, and I was a better communicator. It was thrilling to discover that I could study and absorb new information. I had not had that experience in my childhood—and surely not as a teen. It seemed to be a blessing that the Lord delayed that opportunity until I could deeply appreciate it. I enjoyed many of my classes, such as children's literature and art, microbiology, astronomy, and Portuguese, which I had spoken as a little girl when our family served a mission in Brazil.

My last semester was something of a crucible. It was a typically cold Utah winter, and right at midterm, our ward was divided. In the ward division, I lost both counselors and 15 primary teachers. That same week our son came down with ear infections and pneumonia. I missed more than a week of school just taking care of my family and the heavy needs of life. At the end of that week, I was exhausted and critically behind in my schoolwork. I was not prepared for midterm exams, and I had a number of papers and assignments to complete. The effort to catch up seemed almost impossible. When the alarm rang early on the Monday I was to return to school, I turned it off and mumbled into my pillow, "I quit!" My husband, who usually slept through my morning exit, sat up and said, "What?!? I've worked too hard for this degree. Get up and go to school!"

Somehow I finished all that I needed to do for midterms. Our son recovered, the ward was reorganized, and I continued through the rest of the semester. On my last day on campus, after I took my microbiology final, there was a mist of a rain falling, slightly obscuring the *Y* on the mountain. I thought, "The heavens are weeping for joy with me. We did it!" It was a wonderful moment.

LESSONS LEARNED

And now, like Adam and Eve, I have looked back on my mortal experience. It certainly has been different from what I imagined it would be, but I wouldn't change it. What are some of the lessons I learned from my experiences at Dixie College and BYU?

- **Keep moving.** Life is a battle against inertia. This one physical law applies to so much in life. Starting is always more difficult than continuing. Tasks do not complete themselves. Big projects can best be accomplished by breaking them into smaller more approachable portions, but we have to keep moving. When we begin taking a few small steps, we can take other small steps. By working at a goal a little at a time, we come closer to the desired result. The simplest way to complete a goal is to keep working on it. The fastest way to the finish line is to keep going.

- **Prioritize.** In life we wrestle with priorities. Some people prioritize by choosing between *good, better,* and *best.* For me, it is easier to choose between things that are *nice to do,* things that are *necessary,* and things that are *essential.* When we take time every day for the things that are essential to our spiritual well-being—which means that we are on our knees in prayer, we are spending time in the scriptures, and we are repenting every day—then we are focusing on the things that will increase our faith in God. The necessary things will always be dominant in our lives. Just as Adam and Eve worked to earn their bread, we all must take care of physical, financial, and emotional needs. There is a great deal of work that goes into living and being self-reliant: wages to earn, food to be purchased and prepared, homes and belongings to be organized and cared for. We accept Church callings, and we have obligations to family members and duties in our communities. We cannot shirk opportunities to serve and the long list of necessary things to do without falling behind and becoming disorganized. Most of us also have a personal list of things that are nice to do—things we enjoy doing, things that bring pleasure and relaxation to our lives. I have learned that when we focus first on essentials and then the list of necessary things to do, there is almost always time to enjoy many things that are nice to do.
- **Accept help.** Because there will always be challenges, two heads working on a problem is almost always better than

one. Teamwork gives the most beleaguered person an advantage. I was able to complete my part of our family goal only because I received much help from others. It was a blessing to receive help to lighten my load, and over the years I have had my own opportunities to help others in return.

- **Focus on goals.** It is worthwhile to set worthy goals, even if they seem almost impossible. The challenges of life will continue to happen, whether we set and work toward goals or not. Challenges come when we are serving; they come when least expected and never at a convenient time. We just need to work our way through interruptions and continue, as soon as possible, to move ahead with what we hope to accomplish.

- **Learn new things.** We can always expand our interests and develop new skills. A lack of proficiency or talent should not diminish our enjoyment of new endeavors. We are never too old to keep learning, and there is no end to the process of discovering new things and gaining new knowledge. The thirst for knowledge is inspiring and fortifying. It can be a pleasure to expand our perspective and increase our understanding.

- **Be happy now.** We should always try to be happy. We should pray to be happy. We know we're going to be happy in the end, so we can save time by just working at being happy now. My parents established a family motto: "Enjoy It!" They said that we will typically look back on our challenging experiences, talk about them, marvel at them, and even laugh about them. If we are going to enjoy those experiences later, we might as well enjoy and appreciate them now.[4]

- **Seek the Holy Ghost.** With the companionship of the Holy Ghost, our minds can be quickened. We can remember things we study sincerely. We can feel peace amid turmoil.

We can be inspired with sudden answers and comforted when all does not go as we hope it will. With the Holy Ghost, we are more than the sum of our own intelligence.

• **Rely on Heavenly Father and Jesus Christ.** Finally, we all need our Heavenly Father and our Savior in every part of our lives. Because of Them, we can pray for miracles and expect them. Without Them, our puny efforts will never be enough. Because of the Savior's atoning power and through the covenants we honor with Him and our Father, we can depend on strength that is greater than our own during our mortal experience. We don't know all that will occur in our future, but we do know that we are not powerless and that we do not have to travel this experience alone.

As we contemplate our time on the earth, it does not take long to realize that we do not control all our experiences. We cannot control other people. We cannot control most of our circumstances—the natural processes of human bodies or the events of the world. However, we can take responsibility for our choices—the goals we set and how we approach them. We can receive strength through keeping our covenants. We are promised the companionship of the Holy Ghost and the blessings of the Atonement of Christ to lift us. As we journey through our mortal experience, we can have an adventure we did not foresee at the beginning—an adventure that will shape us into people who are grander than we ever envisioned we could be.

Notes

1. See Moses 5:10.
2. See Moses 5:11.
3. See 1 Kings 17:8–16.
4. See Geraldine Hamblin Bangerter, "Enjoy It!" *Ensign,* June 1991, 45.

7

Tender Trials and Assuring Answers

Samuel InJae Shin, a beloved member of our extended family, died tragically in a rock climbing accident in August 2016. We have enjoyed a sweet and close relationship with Samuel's family since his older brother Danny married our daughter Heidi, and we experienced the details of that traumatic event along with Samuel's family. Samuel was vibrant and full of life, and his death shocked and saddened everyone who knew him. Although he was only 28 years old, he had distinguished himself as a neuroscience researcher, and he had a bright future before him. When Brother and Sister Shin asked me to share my testimony of the plan of salvation at Samuel's funeral, I pondered, with fresh eyes and a broken heart, important principles and doctrine about our purpose on the earth. As I thought about our grandchildren, some of whom are Samuel's nieces and nephews, I wanted to answer their new questions about life and death, comfort their tender hearts, and help them learn that mortality is a step in fulfilling our eternal purpose.

❦

It is impossible to go through this life without experiencing the sting of death and parting with people we love and who are close to us. At some point, each of us faces the loss of people who are young or the loss of people who are close to us, and we all get to have our hearts changed by these times. President Thomas S. Monson observed: "Among all the facts of mortality, none is so certain as its end. Death comes to all. . . . It inevitably represents a painful loss of association and, particularly in the young, a crushing blow to dreams unrealized, ambitions unfulfilled, and hopes vanquished."[1]

At times like these—when someone we love so much dies, when we see the promise of an intelligent, contributing person suddenly leave us—we cannot help but reflect on who we are, why we are on the earth, what is fair or unfair, and what constitutes a full life. It is good for us to ask these questions and draw nearer to God for our answers, to seek a renewal of hope and confirm our faith.

THE PLAN

I have come to believe for myself that we had a life before we came to the earth. We call it our pre-earth life. That pre-earth life is also called the first estate—or our first state of being. In that life, we were spirit children of heavenly parents. We were taught lessons in that world, and we rejoiced to learn of our potential. We were given the opportunity to choose to have a mortal experience. Everyone who is on the earth today chose to be born and become mortal. Each of us wanted to receive a physical body to house our spirit so that we could become like our Father in Heaven and eventually receive all the blessings He has. It was a big opportunity, and we were excited about it.

Our mortal life, or earth life, is called the second estate. Our goal in receiving a body was to prepare us to be "fit companions of the Gods and Holy Ones."[2] We rejoiced at the prospect of living with our Father in Heaven forever. When we came to the earth, we became subject to illness, pain, choice, happiness, and natural consequences of the world we were born into. We became subject to temptations, sins, frailties, and challenges put in our way by Satan and his helpers, who rejected the chance to have a mortal body. With our birth came the certainty that this mortal life was temporary and that at some point, the body we had received to carry us through our second estate would die.

To compensate for our weakness and to ensure that our death would not be permanent, we were promised a Savior. Jesus Christ was chosen to mark the path and lead the way back to our heavenly home.[3] He would conquer death and lead us into life eternal.[4] The scriptures today record the life and ministry of Jesus, and we have the testimony of many witnesses of His resurrection and life. We have "hope through the atonement of Christ and the power of his resurrection, to be raised unto life eternal, and this because of [our] faith in him according to the promise."[5]

WHAT IS MORTALITY FOR, AND WHEN IS IT COMPLETE?

At the death of someone as young and vibrant and bright and contributing as Samuel, sometimes people ask if his life was too short or if it is fair that he did not get more time in mortality. When my father, Elder William Grant Bangerter, was close to finishing his time on the earth, he spent some time with me, reflecting on his life. Unlike Samuel, he had lived a long life. He asked me, "Why are we on the earth?" He answered his own question. He said, "We are here to develop ourselves and build the kingdom of God!"

One of the ways we improve ourselves is to make and keep covenants with God that bind us to Jesus Christ as our promised Savior and commit us to be His disciples, trying to do the things he would have us do as His joint-heirs and representatives. Those covenants help us keep repenting and changing in order to become more like Him.

They connect us to Him so we can receive His power to help us overcome challenges and difficulties and live above the temptations and pitfalls that are natural in the world.

THE MEASURE

So, is there a way to know if we are doing what we are supposed to do with our time on the earth? My father taught about "three inspired statements" found in the scriptures that can help us measure our lives:

"1. 'Pure religion and undefiled before God and the Father is this, To visit the fatherless and widows in their affliction, and to keep himself unspotted from the world' (James 1:27).

"2. 'And what doth the Lord require of thee, but to do justly, and to love mercy, and to walk humbly with thy God?' (Micah 6:8).

"3. 'Let us hear the conclusion of the whole matter. Fear God, and keep his commandments: for this is the whole duty of man' (Ecclesiastes 12:13)."[6]

Based on what I know about Samuel's life, I feel confident that he was striving to achieve those measures. By doing so, he was living as a disciple of the Savior, who said, "This is life eternal, that they might know thee the only true God, and Jesus Christ, whom thou hast sent."[7]

WHAT HAPPENS IN THE NEXT LIFE?

Now that Samuel has completed his second estate, where is he, and what is he doing? Because he was faithful, we can be confident that he is among those who "shall have glory added upon their heads for ever and ever."[8] Samuel is most likely one of the Lord's missionaries in the spirit world. We learn in the scriptures that the Lord has "organized his forces and appointed messengers, clothed with power and authority, and commissioned them to go forth and carry the light of the gospel to them that [are] in darkness, even to all the spirits of men."[9]

All the talents and spiritual gifts we work diligently to acquire in this life and all the things we do to improve ourselves will still be part of us when we die. Just as we work to build the Lord's kingdom here, we will continue to build it in the world of spirits. If we have developed gifts of compassion, service, humor, diligence, honesty, trustworthiness, thoughtfulness, and faithfulness in this life, we will continue to use those gifts to bless others in the next.

What Do We Do Now?

Just as Samuel gave abundantly to others and served with enjoyment, we can share our talents and grow in righteousness. We can be more patient, more loving, more understanding. We can focus on relationships and happiness in family life, which can be eternal. To be successful, these relationships must be "established and maintained on principles of faith, prayer, repentance, forgiveness, respect, love, compassion, work, and wholesome recreational activities."[10] We are to continue to be disciples of the Lord Jesus Christ by participating with Him in His work of salvation. By doing so, we will receive peace, happiness, joy, answers to our most difficult questions, and the ability to go forward in tough times. And we are promised that we can receive help from the Holy Ghost as our constant companion. We can rely on Him to comfort and sustain us. And we hold on tight to the great promise of eternal life because our Savior Jesus Christ conquered death so we all might live again.

Notes

1. Thomas S. Monson, "He Is Risen!" *Ensign,* May 2010, 87.
2. Eliza R. Snow, address to Lehi Ward Relief Society, Oct. 27, 1869, Lehi Ward, Alpine (Utah) Stake, in Relief Society, Minute Book, 1868–79,

Church History Library, Salt Lake City, 26; quoted in Julie B. Beck, "And upon the Handmaids in Those Days Will I Pour out My Spirit," *Ensign*, May 2010, 12.

3. See Eliza R. Snow, "How Great the Wisdom and the Love," *Hymns* (1985), no. 195.

4. See John 14:6; 17:3; Mosiah 16:7–8; Marion D. Hanks, "That Easter Morn," *Hymns,* no. 198; John A. Widtsoe, "Lead Me into Life Eternal," *Hymns,* no. 45.

5. Moroni 7:41.

6. William Grant Bangerter, *The Collected Works of William Grant Bangerter: Speeches and Presentations Made as a General Authority of The Church of Jesus Christs of Latter-day Saints* (2008), 451–52.

7. John 17:3.

8. Abraham 3:26.

9. Doctrine and Covenants 138:30.

10. "The Family: A Proclamation to the World," *Ensign,* Nov. 2010, 129.

PIONEERS, PROMISES, AND PLANTING

Evidence of Faith, Assurance of Hope

One of my greatest joys is traveling with grandchildren. It is especially fascinating to see their unique natures emerge when they are away from parents, siblings, and friends. As my husband and I planned a trip with our three oldest grandsons, we created a syllabus of important places to visit and principles to teach. We hoped to help them concentrate on their purpose on the earth and on their responsibility as priesthood bearers. This was their season to prepare for eternal covenant keeping—a time to secure their testimonies, solidify their conversion to the gospel, and prepare to serve missions. During our studies together on that trip, we all felt an increase in faith and a greater sense of our identity. The truths we learned became part of my message about family and covenants at the Reason for Hope conference at Brigham Young University in November 2017.

My husband and I once visited one of the most respected planetariums in the United States to hear a lecture about the night sky. An experienced astronomer taught us about constellations and about the Cassini mission, which involved a probe sent to take pictures of

Saturn. After her lecture, she answered questions from the audience. Many of the questions centered on how far into space we have been able to probe. People asked how far away the nearest galaxy is, if any signs of life have been discovered in other galaxies, and how much we really know about what is in the far distances of space.

After listening to the astronomer's answers for almost an hour, I, an admitted novice, was amazed by how many of her explanations seemed to be a combination of mathematics, physics, and some guesswork. I was astonished that after spending billions of dollars and thousands of years studying the heavens, mankind had found so few concrete answers about anything outside of our solar system.

I have thought since about my belief regarding the heavens and how things were created and how I gained that understanding. I have wondered how much I would know if I relied only upon science. I have realized that if that were my only way to gain knowledge, I would always come up short of what I really want to know.

I have concluded that although I can learn some very interesting things in a planetarium, I will never find the answers to my most important questions there. I am akin to Alma, who testified that "all things denote there is a God; yea, even the earth, and all things that are upon the face of it, yea, and its motion, yea, and also all the planets which move in their regular form do witness that there is a Supreme Creator."[1]

HOPE AND FAITH

I have reflected seriously about how I came to know who God is. How have I learned His attributes? How have I learned to have faith in Him and His promises? How have I learned about my Savior Jesus Christ, His mission and His miracles? How have I gained a testimony of His restored gospel? How have I learned to not be derailed by the imperfections I have seen in myself and other servants in the Lord's Church? How have I learned my own purpose? How have I found answers to the questions of why and what and how? How have I found the strength to push through difficulties in my life and cope with punishing challenges in a spirit of faith?

During my formative years, my parents taught me that it was my responsibility to nurture my faith. They presented the gospel of Jesus Christ to me in beautiful and powerful ways, and then they helped me use my questions to gain my own faith and understanding. I have learned for myself, though prayer, fasting, study, service, desire, and experience, that "faith is the assurance of things hoped for, the evidence of things not seen."[2]

Over the years, my certainty has grown that we have a Heavenly Father. He has a plan for us. His Beloved Son, our Savior Jesus Christ, plays the central role in carrying out this plan. We can have constant access to the Holy Ghost, the third member of the Godhead, as a daily Prompter and Guide. I have a knowledge that the gospel has been restored and that all priesthood ordinances and covenants necessary for us to return to dwell with our Heavenly Father are restored in The Church of Jesus Christ of Latter-day Saints. This restoration came through Joseph Smith, who received authority to do the work of salvation, and that same authority continues today in priesthood keys held by a living prophet. This is more than a guess for me. It is a priceless collection of "evidence" I have worked hard to assemble. It is in my soul. It is a knowledge achieved through study and faith. It is now like a tree I have nourished that has grown to fill my life.[3]

I have learned much about faith—that I need more of it and that as I exercise it with more power, I will be blessed. I have learned much about "hope through the atonement of Christ."[4] I can't package my faith and hope and give it to you, nor can I give half of it to you and keep half for myself. So I invite you to join me on three journeys of "assurance of things hoped for" and "evidence of things not seen." My desire is that these journeys will inspire you to plant your own seed of faith or to nourish the faith you already have. Ultimately, that seed can become an ever-growing tree for you.

PIONEERS

Our first journey is about pioneers. As I ponder the lives of pioneers in my family, I am inspired by their hope and faith in Christ, by their testimony of Joseph Smith's prophetic mission, and by their determination to keep their covenants.

In July 2017, while my husband and I were traveling to a family reunion, our vehicle lost its power steering, necessitating a stop in Lyman, Wyoming, a small town on the windy expanse of the Bridger Valley. It so happens that a number of my ancestors were homesteaders in that valley and are buried in Lyman. And so, while we were there for repairs, we went to the cemetery and looked for their graves. A couple of them were easy to find, and some were obscure little markers almost buried in the grass.

The two smallest and least cared-for headstones marked the graves of my ancestors James Henry Rollins and Evaline Walker Rollins, early members of the Church. James's young widowed mother was baptized near Palmyra, New York, shortly after the Church was organized in 1830. With her and his two sisters, Mary Elizabeth and Caroline, James later traveled to Kirtland, Ohio, where as a teen, he lived with and worked for Joseph and Emma Smith. Then he went on to Missouri, where he was a friend and defender of the Prophet and was arrested and imprisoned with many other faithful Saints in Far West. In Missouri, James's sisters saved pages of the Doctrine and Covenants from a burning print shop. Later, as newlyweds, he and his wife, Evaline, walked through snow to reach refuge in what became Nauvoo, Illinois. James and Evaline established their household next to Joseph and Emma Smith's home, and James helped build the Nauvoo Temple. He and Evaline later traveled west with the Saints. They were part of a mission to settle San Bernardino, California, and they also helped establish communities in Utah. Eventually they died in Lyman, Wyoming, in the cabin of their daughter and son-in-law.

Also in Lyman are the graves of my ancestors George and Rebecca Eyre. George emigrated from England with his brother and parents. His mother died early in the journey, and he watched as she was sent to her grave in the Atlantic Ocean. He later saw his father die on the plains of Wyoming, a few days short of the Salt Lake Valley.

I later stopped in Minersville, Utah, another little-known town settled by my ancestors. There I found the grave of the mother and sisters of James Henry Rollins. I also found the graves of my great-great-grandparents Oscar and Mary Ann Hamblin, who went with Oscar's brother Jacob on a mission of peace to the Native American people in southern Utah. Daphne Hamblin, their mother, had died way back on the pioneer trail in Mt. Pisgah, Iowa, at a camp where some of the Saints stopped to regroup after being driven out of Nauvoo. In southern Utah, the Hamblin family suffered greatly from heat, privation, starvation, flash floods, and illness. Oscar and Jacob buried their father on a bluff above what is now Santa Clara, Utah, and Oscar died soon after that, at the age of 29, of a disease he contracted while serving his mission.

In Murray, Utah, I visited the graves of my great-great-grandparents Henry and Ann Bawden, who left a verdant valley in England to join the Saints in Utah. I also found the graves of my great-grandparents Frederick and Maria Bangerter, who fled religious persecution in Switzerland in order to rear their children in Zion.

Additionally, I live on the back slopes of "cemetery hill" in Alpine, Utah, where my ancestors named Carlisle and Freestone are buried. I frequently visit the graves of those early Alpine settlers to contemplate their sacrifices and enduring faith.

These few ancestors are representative of others—such as William Wood, who marched with the Mormon Battalion, and Elizabeth Walmsley, who took her 10 living children to the St. George Temple to be sealed to her and her deceased husband soon after it was dedicated. I have been inspired and blessed to learn more about these people, and I have developed a deep love and respect for them. To me they have assumed heroic stature because of their love and sacrifice for the gospel of Jesus Christ.

Of my 32 great-great-great-grandparents, 23 lived in the generation who first heard the message of the restored gospel. All of those who heard those principles and doctrines joined the Church. In the next generation, 13 of my 16 great-great grandparents faithfully made and kept covenants, and the remaining 3 did not have the opportunity to do so. All 8 of my great-grandparents made and kept covenants throughout their lives. My 4 grandparents were exemplary covenant keepers, passing their heritage to my parents, who were my earliest teachers and my lifelong examples.

As I have pondered their lives, I have asked myself, "Is there any reason to doubt their sincerity and faith? Could it be possible that 100 percent of those who accepted the gospel in the early days of the Restoration were deluded, ignorant, manipulated, naïve, trapped, confused, misled, or crazy? Did they all suffer and endure privation and challenges just because they didn't have other options? Were they too poor to do anything else?" I cannot believe that to be so. Their stories tell me that they were skilled, innovative, adventurous, tenacious, informed, strong-minded, and widely experienced. I have not found a record of one of them questioning the reality of God or complaining about why He would allow His children to suffer.

I have wondered—if they lived today, would they continue in their faith in a world awash in diverse opinions and saturated with conflicting information? Would these people, who were driven from homes and persecuted in several states and countries, retain their faith now? Could they withstand the jibes, the snickers, the misinformation, the fun at our expense, the misunderstandings, the outright lies, and the persistent public caricatures about us that continue to this day? Would these people, who interacted with Joseph Smith, who knew him as an extraordinary and steady man, who were acquainted with his character, gifts, and capacity and also his imperfections, be swayed by claims that he was a false prophet? Would my ancestors, who believed him to be inspired, who wept when he was murdered, still weep for him now? After the sum of their experiences, would they still follow his successor, Brigham Young, into the wilderness and certain adversity? Would they maintain their great hope in their covenants and the power of the priesthood, and would they continue to feel the power of the Holy Ghost in their lives? I believe they would.

I remember that my Grandpa Hamblin, as an older man, wept as he recounted listening to his grandmother Evaline tell him stories in their cabin about her experiences in Missouri and Nauvoo. She knew Joseph Smith well and made the long journey to settle in the West under the direction of Brigham Young. The memory of her faith burned in his heart, and he, in his simple way, tried to pass that same feeling on to his children and grandchildren. I have thought that for me to become a weak link in that powerful chain of faith would be the ultimate display of ingratitude, the most selfish and painful rejection of their legacy. Even now, their stories inspire me and challenge me and lift me above the sophistry and complexity of the present day.

The point of mentioning these people is not to boast about my connection to early Church pioneers. It is not to say that everyone in my family line was perfect in keeping the commandments all the time. It is the perfection of the covenants, not the people, that is important.

After these people had learned of the restored gospel and partaken of the blessings of their covenants, they did not abandon or reject them. Their covenants provided deep roots that have nurtured my own tree of faith. I now have the responsibility to carry the faith of my ancestors to my own new branches, my own posterity. As the covenants of my forefathers have been roots for me, I have a duty to continue their legacy by becoming the fruit of their sacrifice and commitment.

I have many friends who are pioneers themselves—the first in their families to embrace these covenants. I have other friends who are reestablishing the covenants in their families after others have not kept them. Every covenant keeper is essential in a tree of faith. As they make and honor the covenants and then pass them to others, they share immeasurable blessings.

PROMISES

Our second journey is about promises.

In 2017 my husband and I took our three teenage grandsons to visit some early Church history and cultural sites, with a goal to strengthen our understanding of the priesthood and give context to help them prepare for missions. We wanted to learn more about the Lord's promises to His covenant people and be strengthened in our determination to qualify for those promises. Our hope was that we would increase our faith in Jesus Christ and in His assurance that He will help us in our earthly journey.

In preparation for the trip, we asked the boys to memorize one scripture passage—section 2 of the Doctrine and Covenants:

"Behold, I will reveal unto you the Priesthood, by the hand of Elijah the prophet, before the coming of the great and dreadful day of the Lord.

"And he shall plant in the hearts of the children the promises made to the fathers, and the hearts of the children shall turn to their fathers.

"If it were not so, the whole earth would be utterly wasted at his coming."[5]

In 1823, on the night of September 21 and the morning of September 22, the angel Moroni visited Joseph Smith four times and taught Joseph about his mission and the Restoration of the gospel. Each time, Moroni made the declaration that is now quoted in Doctrine and Covenants 2. This passage is similar to a prophecy recorded in the book of Malachi and in other places in the scriptures.[6] For Joseph Smith and for us, these verses help establish the foundation of all we believe.

On our trip with our grandsons, we studied different aspects of these verses. In discussions spread out over several days, we learned much about our identity and purpose.

We learned that in the first verse, the word *I* refers to Jesus Christ. The Lord Jesus Christ is speaking, announcing the restoration of His Father's covenant to the earth. We studied about our Savior's life and mission, His miracles, and His obedience to His Father.

We talked about revelation—who receives it for the Church, who receives it for us personally, and how to qualify for it.

We learned that "through the Prophet Joseph Smith, the priesthood of God has been restored to the earth in its fulness. The priesthood is the eternal power and authority of God by which He blesses, redeems, and exalts His children, bringing to pass 'the immortality and eternal life of man.'"[7]

We learned that "all Heavenly Father's sons and daughters are equally blessed as they draw upon the power of the priesthood."[8]

We learned that "Elijah held the sealing power of the Melchizedek Priesthood. . . . The power of Elijah is the sealing power of the priesthood by which things bound or loosed on earth are bound or loosed in heaven."[9] We learned that Elijah committed the keys of this power to Joseph Smith[10] and that through this restored power, we have access to all the ordinances and blessings of the priesthood that were given to families anciently. Our study of promises gave us new understanding of the prophet Elijah and his mission to plant the promises of eternal blessings in our hearts and how these happy promises generate the seeds of faith we nurture within ourselves.

We asked about the "fathers" mentioned in verse 2. Who are they? We stopped at the Metropolitan Museum of Art in New York City and studied artifacts from Egypt. We looked at sarcophagi, papyri, and vases depicting ancient people. We discussed our spiritual "fathers," such as Abraham, Isaac, Jacob (or Israel), and Joseph, and our ancient mothers, such as Sarah and Rebekah.

We learned about other ancient fathers and mothers, such as Adam and Eve, who understood the nature of God, feared and loved Him, knew His commandments, and lived His laws. They knew that they were "not left without intelligence, or understanding, to wander in darkness, and spend an existence in ignorance and doubt."[11] They knew that "though man did transgress, his transgression did not deprive him of the previous knowledge with which he was endowed, relative to the existence and glory of his Creator."[12] This knowledge was "disseminated among them; so that the existence of God became an object of faith, in the early age of the world," and this "stirred up the faith of multitudes to feel after him; to search after a knowledge of his character, perfections and attributes, until they became extensively acquainted with him; and not only commune with him, and behold his glory, but be partakers of his power, and stand in his presence."[13]

We spent some time talking about the promises made to the fathers. We learned what the promises are and how we can seek those same blessings. We learned that these promises have been passed down through the generations of the ancients. They are administered by the priesthood, which "continueth in the church of God in all generations, and is without beginning of days or end of years. . . . It continueth and abideth forever," and it holds "the key of the mysteries of the kingdom, even the key of the knowledge of God. Therefore, in the ordinances thereof, the power of godliness is manifest. And without the ordinances thereof, and the authority of the priesthood, the power of godliness is not manifest unto men in the flesh; for without this no man can see the face of God, even the Father, and live." We learned that Moses, who loved the promises, "plainly taught [this] to the children of Israel in the wilderness."[14]

We learned that the Aaronic Priesthood holds "the key of . . . the preparatory gospel," which is "the gospel of repentance and of baptism, and of the remission of sins."[15]

We learned about other promises given to the fathers and mothers and to us: that if we "abide in [the Lord's] covenant," we will "inherit thrones, kingdoms, principalities, and powers, dominions, all heights and depths." These blessings come "in time, and through all eternity; and shall be of full force when [we] are out of the world." Our "glory shall be a fulness and a continuation of the seeds forever and ever, . . . both in the world and out of the world,"[16] and we will "have glory added upon [our] heads for ever and ever."[17] "This is eternal lives," the Lord said, "to know the only wise and true God, and Jesus Christ, whom he hath sent."[18]

On the last day of our trip, we finished our study by testifying that if the promises made to the fathers are not planted in the hearts of the children—or in other words, in us—then the Savior's purpose and mission is unfulfilled in them. For those who reject the promises, the mortal experience and the opportunity to receive those promises is "utterly wasted."[19] When I contemplate the depth and breadth of the promises revealed through Elijah, I, like the ancient fathers and mothers and my pioneer ancestors, desire to possess them completely.

PLANTING

Our third journey is about planting.

I found myself on this journey when a granddaughter and I spent a few weeks sifting through documents, pictures, and papers that represented the lives of my father-in-law and mother-in-law, J. Paul Beck and June Strong Beck. For several weeks, we digitized their records and labeled and preserved hundreds of photographs, letters, and artifacts. As we worked, I was struck by how quickly their lives had gone by, what powerful teachers they were, and how diligently they worked to pass along the promises they so richly enjoyed and the legacy of faith they acquired.

J. Paul experienced a troubled upbringing, followed by traumatic service in the United States Navy in World War II. He then spent 40 years working at a steel mill. It was demanding labor. He served privately by repairing cars and lawn mowers for countless friends and neighbors and never avoided a welfare farm assignment. Perhaps because he worked on so many Sundays at the steel mill, he never held a leadership position of any kind in the Church. But his large physical stature was matched by his spiritual stature. He was a perennial teacher of youth. They loved his humor and frankness, and even now, as adults, they can repeat the stories and examples he taught.

June, a lifelong homemaker and Relief Society leader, never lived outside the small town of Alpine, Utah, except for a one-year mission after she was widowed. She was exact in her financial records and a strict tithe payer. Though she was curious about the world, she had a simple understanding of it. Together, she and J. Paul enjoyed seeing the wonders of nature in the school bus that they converted into a camper, traveling as far as their finances would allow. They were an extremely happy couple and had an unusually sweet and devoted life-long romance. And as is normal, life was not always fair for June and J. Paul. They had their share of suffering and a robust mortal experience, which tutored and humbled them.

Early one morning, as was her habit, June was cooking breakfast for one of her sons. As they were alone in the quiet kitchen, she asked him what he was doing about preparing for a mission. He replied that he was not sure he wanted to serve a mission and that he was not convinced the Church was true. Without a pause, June, who tended to be meek and soft spoken, stood up to her much taller son. Thumping him on the chest, she said, with power and authority derived from her own covenant keeping, "Well! If you don't know by now, then it is time you found out! And I want to tell you that I know it's true! If you will try, you will find the same testimony I have!" Humbled, he pondered for days about the power of his mother's testimony and came to the conclusion that he would have to learn for himself. Now a grandfather, he is still emotional when he expresses his gratitude for a mother who was empowered by the Holy Ghost to testify of her knowledge and plant a seed of faith in him.

Alma taught about the process of developing our own faith when he compared the word of God to a seed. He said that faith in our Savior and His promises requires only "a particle of faith" in the beginning. He told his listeners—and us—to make a place for that seed, the word of God, and to not cast it out through unbelief but to give it a chance to "swell" within us, to "enlarge" our souls and "enlighten" our understanding. He testified that if we do this, the seed will bring forth other seeds like it. Our minds will "begin to expand," and our faith will become discernible, take root, and bring forth fruit.[20]

When June and J. Paul passed out of this life, we did not receive a sudden windfall of cash. They did, however, leave a treasure trove of faith to their posterity. They had invested in hard work and thrift, in teaching their children the gospel, in service and compassion, in happy family memories, and in a lifetime of discipleship. June and J. Paul are two people who truly planted seeds of faith and reaped the blessings of those seeds.

POWERFUL FAITH THROUGH THE GIFT AND POWER OF THE HOLY GHOST

Through my journeys of pioneers, promises, and planting, I have learned that faith is "the moving cause of all action" in us.[21] Strong faith grows out of a strong belief in God and the knowledge of His hand in our lives. Faith is the fruit of our own desires and efforts to draw closer to God. We increase our faith through a lifetime, by seeking the rich promises made to our ancient fathers and by making and staying true to our covenants with the Lord.

Faith is "not only the principle of action, but of power, also."[22] It becomes powerful only through the gift and power of the Holy Ghost, who testifies of truth and confirms our faith. My father taught this important principle through the example of the Apostle Peter. Although Peter witnessed the miracles of Jesus and participated with Him as a faithful disciple, at a time of severe trial he was not strong enough to acknowledge that he was one of Jesus's followers. At that time in his life, he was weak when the Savior was not with him. However, after the day of Pentecost, when Peter received the Holy Ghost, he was a very strong Peter. Daddy said: "Never again in his whole life did he ever waver from his mission. He was able to suffer imprisonment, punishment, to withstand temptation, and finally to be delivered up to death for the testimony that he had received."[23]

The key to powerful faith is having the Spirit always with us so we can withstand the attacks of the adversary. Satan is waging war against the faithful. He is opportunistic, like a virus or bacteria, waiting to begin an infection at a sign of weakness. It is easy to fall under the influence of an unhappy spirit—to wallow in darkness, discouragement, anger, blame, apathy, and entitlement. But the Lord has given us this counsel and promise:

"Put your trust in that Spirit which leadeth to do good—yea, to do justly, to walk humbly, to judge righteously; and this is my Spirit.

"Verily, verily, I say unto you, I will impart unto you of my Spirit, which shall enlighten your mind, which shall fill your soul with joy."[24]

My great-great-grandfather Oscar Hamblin's brother Jacob taught how this principle operated when he had just a particle of faith. The night he first heard a missionary teach the restored gospel, he said to himself, "How shall I know whether or not these things are so, and be satisfied?" Immediately after Jacob thought that, the missionary stood and said, "'If there is anyone in the congregation who wishes to know how he can satisfy himself of the truth of these things, I can assure him that if he will be baptized, and have hands laid upon him for the gift of the Holy Ghost, he shall have an assurance of their truth.'"

Jacob later recounted, "This so fired up my mind, that I at once determined to be baptized, and that too, if necessary, at the sacrifice of the friendship of my kindred and of every earthly tie." But his resolution wavered as he walked to the place where he was to be baptized. He recalled: "As my pace slackened, some person seemed to come from above, who I thought was my [deceased] grandfather. He seemed to say to me, 'Go on, my son; your heart cannot deceive, neither has it entered into your mind to imagine the blessings that are in store for you, if you go on and continue in this work.' I lagged no more, but hurried to the pool where I was baptized."[25]

In this spirit and in the name of Jesus Christ, I testify of the amazing blessings that are in store for us as we move forward and remain faithful. I am grateful for the influence of pioneers, promises, and planting. This is an assurance of hope. This is evidence of things not seen.

Notes

1. Alma 30:44.
2. JST, Hebrews 11:1.
3. See Alma 32.
4. Moroni 7:41.
5. Doctrine and Covenants 2:1–3.
6. See Malachi 4:5–6; see also 3 Nephi 25:5–6; Doctrine and Covenants 110:14–15; Joseph Smith–History 1:36–39.
7. *Daughters in My Kingdom: The History and Work of Relief Society* (2011), 127; quoting Moses 1:39.
8. *Daughters in My Kingdom,* 127.
9. Bible Dictionary, "Elijah," 664.
10. See Doctrine and Covenants 110:13–16.
11. *Lectures on Faith,* 2:18, in the introductory material of the 1835 edition of the Doctrine and Covenants, 15; available at josephsmithpapers.org /paper-summary/doctrine-and-covenants-1835/23; accessed 19 April 2018.
12. *Lectures on Faith,* 2:19, in the introductory material of the 1835 edition of the Doctrine and Covenants, 15; available at josephsmithpapers.org /paper-summary/doctrine-and-covenants-1835/23; accessed 19 April 2018.
13. *Lectures on Faith,* 2:33–34, in the introductory material of the 1835 edition of the Doctrine and Covenants, 19; available at josephsmith papers.org/paper-summary/doctrine-and-covenants-1835/27; accessed 19 April 2018.

14. Doctrine and Covenants 84:17–23.
15. Doctrine and Covenants 84:26–27.
16. Doctrine and Covenants 132:19, 30.
17. Abraham 3:26.
18. Doctrine and Covenants 132:24.
19. Doctrine and Covenants 2:3.
20. See Alma 32:27–37.
21. *Lectures on Faith*, 1:10, in the introductory material of the 1835 edition of the Doctrine and Covenants, 6; josephsmithpapers.org/paper-summary/doctrine-and-covenants-1835/14; accessed 19 April 2018.
22. *Lectures on Faith*, 1:13, in the introductory material of the 1835 edition of the Doctrine and Covenants, 7; available at josephsmithpapers.org/paper-summary/doctrine-and-covenants-1835/15; accessed 19 April 2018.
23. William Grant Bangerter, *The Collected Works of William Grant Bangerter: Speeches and Presentations Made as a General Authority of The Church of Jesus Christ of Latter-day Saints* (2008), 469.
24. Doctrine and Covenants 11:12–13.
25. Jacob Hamblin, in Pearson H. Corbett, *Jacob Hamblin, Peacemaker* (1952), 10.

Joyful Labor

"Ye have been diligent in laboring
with me in my vineyard. . . . Behold ye shall
have joy with me because of the
fruit of my vineyard."

—Jacob 5:75

9

LIVING A FRUITFUL LIFE

In April 2013, I spoke to students at Brigham Young University–Idaho about some things I had been studying. I had been thinking about how Adam and Eve had remained faithful even though they did not have access to the scriptures, the words of prophets, and other gospel resources we have in such abundance today. I had thought about how they kept their covenants and fulfilled their purpose so valiantly. I pondered on their faithfulness as I listened to temple ordinances and as I studied the books of Moses, Abraham, and Genesis and other resources. I wanted to distill and assimilate in my own life the simplicity and genius of the commands they were given.

For me, remembering is difficult. Some people have great memories, but mine is leaky. I remember concepts quite well, but I cannot recall a lot of data accurately. And trying to remember names is almost impossible. I find it difficult to remember long and complicated instructions, and I often cannot remember more than five items I need on my shopping list if I do not write them down. Because of this, I appreciate the Lord's instructions to Adam and Eve. He gave them simple commands that they would be able to remember, even after He sent them out of the Garden of Eden and away from His presence.

In Genesis 1 we read, "God blessed them, and God said unto them, Be fruitful, and multiply, and replenish the earth, and subdue it: and have dominion over the fish of the sea, and over the fowl of the air, and over every living thing that moveth upon the earth."[1]

These instructions were simple enough and memorable enough that Adam and Eve could carry them around in their minds and hearts. Perhaps they wrote them down, but even if they didn't, they could remember the Lord and His instructions at every moment. The instructions they received are timeless and still effective in helping us keep our focus on God and His plan for us.

Beginning with the clear direction to *be fruitful*, the Lord provided a way for Adam and Eve to become like Him. I have pondered these simple and memorable instructions, looking for their application in our lives today.

BE FRUITFUL

Fruitfulness is the result of an abundant harvest. It is the product of the long-term labor of sowing, toiling, and reaping. The Lord has often used fruit and fruitfulness as metaphors to teach us what He desires us to become. Ultimately, our lives are the fruit that the Lord gathers into His covenant. One of the most detailed descriptions of this process is found in the allegory recorded in Jacob 5. From this narrative, we learn of the tremendous effort the Lord is willing to expend in order to establish and preserve His covenant family. His covenant-keeping children are the natural fruit, which has been "most precious unto him from the beginning."[2]

In New Testament times, Jesus taught His disciples that "every good tree bringeth forth good fruit"[3] and that people will be known "by their fruits," for good or evil.[4] He shared a parable about a man who sowed seeds in different kinds of ground, teaching that the word of God will be fruitful in us only if our "ground" is good.[5] When we follow the gospel principles of faith and obedience, of repentance and hope and charity, our lives yield abundantly and we become the fruit that the Lord speaks of—that natural, precious fruit.

MULTIPLY

After the Lord instructed Adam and Eve to be fruitful, He gave them additional instructions that help us understand *how* to be fruitful. The first of these is to multiply. The word *multiply* means to increase in number, amount, extent, or degree. Latter-day prophets have said: "The first commandment that God gave to Adam and Eve pertained to their potential for parenthood as husband and wife. We declare that God's commandment for His children to multiply and replenish the earth remains in force."[6]

The Lord's command to marry and to bear and rear children ensures the continuation of His covenant in earthly families. His covenant also continues as we share the gospel and as we do work in temples for ancestors who have died without making covenants. As we participate in the work of salvation, we multiply the number of God's children who make covenants with Him.

The principle of multiplying is applicable in other aspects of our lives as well. The Lord taught this in the parable of the talents. He told of a man who gave talents to three servants. Two of the servants increased what He had given them. The third servant hid his talent and did not increase it. The lord of the servants said that the third man was "wicked and slothful." Commenting on this parable, Jesus said, "Unto every one that hath shall be given, and he shall have abundance: but from him that hath not shall be taken away even that which he hath."[7]

Increasing our talents and multiplying our abilities shows our gratitude to God for the blessings He has given us.

REPLENISH

The word *replenish* means to make full or complete, to resupply or to nourish. Although God's command to "multiply and replenish the earth" refers to covenant-keeping parenthood, there are many other lessons we can learn from this word.

When we take care of our physical bodies, we replenish ourselves. We prolong our lives and make our time on the earth more effective.

Covenant keeping replenishes us. When we partake of the sacrament each week, remembering the Savior and renewing our covenants, we replenish ourselves spiritually.

As we study the scriptures, we feed our spirits and add to our understanding of the Lord. When we "teach one another the doctrine of the kingdom,"[8] we replenish each other. When we learn "of things both in heaven and in the earth, and under the earth; things which have been, things which are, things which must shortly come to pass; things which are at home, things which are abroad; the wars and the perplexities of the nations, and the judgments which are on the land; and . . . also of countries and of kingdoms,"[9] we are replenished. Continual learning and improvement ensures continual replenishment and is a sign of gratitude for our blessings.

SUBDUE

The word *subdue* means to bring under control, to vanquish or conquer. This powerful idea can be tied to our need for the atoning power of the Lord in our lives. In our hearts and minds and in our families and homes, we are expected to subdue all evil influences. We work throughout our lives to subdue unhappy feelings and worries about things that we cannot control. We are to vanquish fear and control our thoughts. We exercise faith in Jesus Christ and His Atonement so we can triumph over adversity and subdue the effects of our weak and fallen nature. King Benjamin taught, "The natural man is an enemy to God, and has been from the fall of Adam, and will be, forever and ever, unless he yields to the enticings of the Holy Spirit, and putteth off the natural man and becometh a saint through the atonement of Christ the Lord, and becometh as a child, submissive, meek, humble, patient, full of love, willing to submit to all things which the Lord seeth fit to inflict upon him, even as a child doth submit to his father."[10]

It was important for Adam and Eve to subdue, or take control over, the earth, meaning that they needed to learn to manage the earth in order to take care of themselves. They had the challenge to subdue every influence that would prevent them from becoming the people their Heavenly Father expected them to become. That challenge continues for us today.

HAVE DOMINION

In the Lord's command to Adam and Eve, the word *dominion* connotes righteous leadership. It means to have authority or sovereignty or ownership. It means to rise above something and master it. After the Lord drove Adam and Eve out of the garden, "Adam began to till the earth, and to have dominion over all the beasts of the field, and to eat his bread by the sweat of his brow. . . . And Eve, also, his wife, did labor with him."[11] But Adam and Eve did more than work the land. They were the spiritual leaders and teachers of their family. Once they had an understanding of the plan of salvation, "they made all things known unto their sons and their daughters."[12] It is our responsibility to teach and lead with love and righteousness in our families.

DRESS AND KEEP

In Genesis 2, we find another instruction from the Lord for Adam and Eve, another expression of fruitful living: "And the Lord God took the man, and put him into the Garden of Eden to dress it and to keep it."[13] To dress is to protect, to adorn, to cultivate. To keep is to maintain in good order, to treasure, defend, and guard. These principles relate to agency and stewardship. They remind me of the Lord's words to the early Saints when He commanded them to build the Kirtland Temple: "Organize yourselves; prepare every needful thing; and establish a house, even a house of prayer, a house of fasting, a house of faith, a house of learning, a house of glory, a house of order, a house of God."[14]

FRUITFUL LIVING

I was raised by a mother and father who understood and applied the command to be fruitful. When my parents got married, they went on a car trip for their honeymoon. They began discussing their family and the culture they wanted in their home. On a paper sack, Mother took notes of their conversation. They asked each other, "What is our family going to be like? What do we want our children to accomplish? Do we want them to be married in the temple? Do we want them to serve missions? Do we want them to receive a university education?" And my father, on his honeymoon, said yes to all these questions. He even said that all their children should take piano lessons. Then my mother and father said, "Well, in order to do all that, we will have family home evening, and we will study the scriptures. We will go to church every week. We will accept callings and serve. We will teach our children the gospel to the best of our ability. We will do the work to teach our children and prepare them for the challenges of life."

Those principles guided our family. When my mother and father established their plan, they didn't know their family would grow to include 10 children. They didn't know the effort it would take to teach their children to work, to see that all had opportunities to learn music, to serve in the Church, and to experience sacrifice and love at home. They could not have foreseen the energy it would require to prepare and send missionaries, to prepare children for temple marriages, to help their children graduate from a university. And then, as the years went by and 65 grandchildren were added, they felt their responsibility increase.

I have always been impressed that my parents made a covenant with the Lord and then they did the work to keep that covenant. They made a plan to multiply, replenish, subdue, have dominion, and to dress and keep—because they had a vision of a fruitful, abundant harvest.

I know that not all people are blessed to grow up in a fruitful home. This does not mean that they cannot keep these principles in their own lives. My father-in-law, who lived in difficult circumstances as a young man, told me several times, "You have two chances for a happy, eternal family. The first one is the one you're born into, and the second one is the one you create. And it's the second one that counts."

"I WILL . . . ESTABLISH MY COVENANT WITH YOU"

When God gave the command to be fruitful, He knew that Adam and Eve would not be perfect in following it, and neither would their posterity. But He provided a way for them to be saved from their imperfections. Adam and Eve learned about the way of salvation as they worshiped God and offered sacrifices, according to the Lord's command:

"After many days an angel of the Lord appeared unto Adam, saying: Why dost thou offer sacrifices unto the Lord? And Adam said unto him: I know not, save the Lord commanded me.

"And then the angel spake, saying: This thing is a similitude of the sacrifice of the Only Begotten of the Father, which is full of grace and truth.

"Wherefore, thou shalt do all that thou doest in the name of the Son, and thou shalt repent and call upon God in the name of the Son forevermore."[15]

We do not know how "many days" Adam and Eve worshiped and sacrificed before they learned these truths. Perhaps they did so for years, not fully understanding why. But their obedience was rewarded. They received greater understanding of the Lord's atoning power. They continued in obedience and received priesthood ordinances and made covenants.[16] They repented of their sins, knowing that He would make up for what they lacked if they would put forth their best efforts. He would intervene with mercy and miracles. He would make their lives fruitful through His redeeming and exalting power.

Like Adam and Eve, we receive the fulness of Jesus Christ's saving power through the priesthood ordinances we receive and the covenants we make and keep, beginning with baptism and the gift of the Holy Ghost. And in the ordinances of the temple, we receive additional instructions and blessings that help us live a fruitful life.

The Lord commanded Adam and Eve and all of us to be fruitful—to multiply, to replenish, to subdue, to have dominion, to dress and keep. These are commandments we can remember. And we have access to the Savior's power and blessings. We can be confident in His help and in His strength. To the ancient Israelites and to us, He said:

"I will have respect unto you, and make you fruitful, and multiply you, and establish my covenant with you. . . .

"And I will walk among you, and will be your God, and ye shall be my people."[17]

NOTES

1. Genesis 1:28.
2. Jacob 5:74.
3. Matthew 7:17.
4. Matthew 7:20; see also verses 17–19.
5. See Matthew 13:3–9, 18–23.
6. "The Family: A Proclamation to the World," *Ensign,* Nov. 2010, 129.
7. Matthew 25:29; see also verses 14–28, 30.
8. Doctrine and Covenants 88:77.
9. Doctrine and Covenants 88:79.
10. Mosiah 3:19.
11. Moses 5:1.
12. Moses 5:12.
13. Genesis 2:15.
14. Doctrine and Covenants 88:119.
15. Moses 5:6–8.
16. See Moses 6:64–66.
17. Leviticus 26:9, 12.

10

"SOMEBODY"
HAS A NAME

Years ago, when a friend lost her son in an accident, I received strong impressions to drop what I was doing and visit her. When I arrived at her home, she asked me how I knew she was praying for me to come. After our visit, I rejoiced that the Lord knew her and answered her prayer. In that moment, the Spirit taught me that when the Lord sent me to her, He showed that He knew me also. In March 2016, as I addressed the President's Leadership Council at Brigham Young University, I spoke to people who had given their time, means, and talents to help build people, the university, and the Church. My message to them was simple. It was a reminder that God knows His children and that one way He shows His love for us is by inspiring us to help each other.

My parents had a saying—we heard it many times as children: "'Somebody' has a name."

When we see something that needs attention, we often say, "Somebody ought to do something about that," "Somebody should fix that," or "Somebody should take care of that." My parents taught me by how they lived that if I am able to help, that "somebody" ought to be me.

OLD CARS AND NEW BOY SCOUTS

In one place where we lived, people were fond of storing old vehicles behind their homes. Old cars were used as storage sheds for camping equipment and gardening tools and so on. City officials hoped that somebody would step forward and lead a city-wide effort to get rid of some of the old cars. So "somebody" volunteered, and it was my mother. The first year, about 75 worn-out cars left town behind tow trucks, and that exodus continued for several years.

Years later, "somebody" was needed to work with Boy Scouts in Portugal, where my father was mission president, so my mother said, "I guess I'm somebody." And she went to work helping boys succeed in Scouting.

My father was equally diligent in seeing needs and taking care of them. He helped widows, gave special attention to missionaries who needed encouragement, and took time to visit friends and neighbors who were ill or in distress. These were mostly quiet, personal acts. I observed only a few of them, but many recipients of my father's watch-care told me about what he did for them.

Over and over I learned, through observing my parents, that "somebody" has a name.

BILLY

When my brother was a Blazer Scout, no one wanted to teach that class of often-unruly boys. My mother said, "I will substitute until you find someone who will accept that calling." She taught that class of 11-year-old boys for approximately 5 years. Now, more than 50 years later, I will occasionally meet a man who tells me of going to my parents' home with other boys, eating waffles, and reviewing his Scouting requirements with my mother. Then, with emotion, he will say, "I earned my Eagle Scout Award because she helped me and cared about my achievement."

During that time, a boy I will call Billy moved into town. His family did not attend church, and his parents smoked. My mom thought Billy would be blessed by participating in her Blazer Scout class, so she went to visit his mother. She asked if he could come to Primary, and when she received an affirmative answer, she told him she would pick him up every week.

Primary was held on a weekday in those days. The first time Billy came to class, the other boys pinched their noses and started making fun of him because he smelled of cigarette smoke. Mother asked Billy to step out in the hall for a minute. Then she said to the other boys, "If I ever, ever see you do anything like that again, I will bring your mothers to Primary every week! Now, Billy is going to come back in, and you are going to be nice. Not just today, but always!" Billy was invited back into the class, and that was that. No more poking fun at Billy!

Mother mentored Billy by saying things like this: "Next week I am going to give a lesson on the such-and-such Article of Faith. Why don't you memorize it so that when I ask questions, you can be the smartest one?" And the next week, when she would ask the boys questions, Billy always knew the right answers.

In time, Mother invited Billy to bring his little brothers and sisters to Primary, and he did. Then she invited them all to come to Sunday School and sacrament meeting and sit with our family.

Just before Billy was to become a deacon, the ward divided, and Billy's family was assigned to the other ward. But he didn't go to that ward. He kept coming to the ward where my mother was, so he could sit with us. Billy's new bishop called my mother one day and said, "That boy is never going to be a deacon because you won't let him go to the ward where he is supposed to go." She replied, "Bishop, when you love Billy like I love Billy, you won't have to beg him to come to your ward."

The bishop took my mother's counsel to heart. Eventually Billy's family moved away, but he continued to advance in the Aaronic Priesthood. He later became an elder and married in the temple. For that to happen, "somebody" had to care and work in an inspired way to mentor him.

EACH OF US CAN BE "SOMEBODY"

I believe we can all develop a lifelong pattern of stepping forward and saying, "Somebody needs to help, and I will do that." Being "somebody" is more than serving in Church callings; it is seeing a need anywhere and filling that need. We might call it discipleship.

The Savior taught a parable about a Samaritan who, as he was traveling, came upon a man who had been robbed and injured and left helpless. The Samaritan helped that man by giving him quick aid and comfort, but he also saw that the injured man received help for a longer recovery.[1] In the latter days, the Savior has said that we should "be anxiously engaged in a good cause, and do many things of [our] own free will, and bring to pass much righteousness."[2] In these and other lessons, the Savior has taught that to follow Him, we are to be "somebody" who can fill a need in a timely way. It is rarely convenient or timely for us. And, as we see in the example of the Good Samaritan, there will probably be no audience to applaud or recognize our service, and there might not be an ecclesiastical assignment to do the work— only the private opportunity.

As I have studied the Bible, I have been drawn to the stories of Rebekah, Esther, Martha, and others who stepped forward to serve and fill special needs at critical times. I love the Book of Mormon accounts of Nephi, Abinadi, Abish, Captain Moroni, Helaman, Teancum, and others who knew the importance of "somebody" stepping forward with faith and courage to take care of difficult needs at critical times. Through these accounts, we learn that for good things to be done in our communities and neighborhoods, "somebody" must step forward and help.

The Lord knows and depends on "somebodies" to do all kinds of things, in our Church callings, in civic service, and as we go about our daily lives. This is service we don't get paid for. We won't often be praised for it. We don't have to do it to be considered worthy and accepted by the Lord—but our help makes a difference. And in making that difference, we follow the Savior's example of going about doing good.[3]

We can tie our knowledge of the restored gospel back to Joseph Smith entering a grove of trees, offering a sincere prayer and asking an honest question. My father often taught in family home evening lessons that when the angel Moroni gave Joseph instructions about receiving and translating ancient scripture, Joseph didn't say, "Oh, no, Mr. Angel! I didn't really want to do all that! I just wanted to know which church to join!" Joseph accepted the responsibility to be the prophet through whom the Lord would restore His covenant to the earth. In doing so, he was "somebody" who did what was needed when it was needed, and out of his faithfulness grew a tremendous amount of truth and good. Through him, we are blessed to have a knowledge of the true, restored gospel of Jesus Christ.

I have seen many examples of people who have stepped forward to help when it was not convenient, when perhaps they needed some help themselves. They stand out to me as people of stature, people who do not make excuses and who have learned how to draw upon the powers of heaven to see needs and then respond. God is aware of all His children, and He knows those who need help. He is also aware when "somebody" *will* help, when "somebody" *will* go. And as those "somebodies" respond, they learn that He knows them also—because He sends them.

NOTES

1. See Luke 10:30–37.
2. Doctrine and Covenants 58:27.
3. See Acts 10:38.

11

HEARING THE
LORD'S VOICE

One interesting life equation for me is that almost as soon as I accept an assignment to speak about or learn about a specific topic, I am confronted with new opportunities to learn about that principle. Such was the case in the spring of 2017, when I accepted an assignment from our stake Relief Society president to teach Relief Society sisters about personal revelation. Immediately I began experiencing various dilemmas that required a great deal of personal revelation. Those situations gave me an opportunity to review what I already knew and to learn truths I still needed to know about this important gift—a gift that helps us be effective in working with the Lord to live His covenant and fulfill our purpose.

When my family was young, I suffered through a long-term illness. For more than a decade, our family situation, our finances, and our spirits were impacted by my poor physical health. I did not sleep well, and I was always trying to minimize pain and discomfort. I tried to do my best every day to ensure that the family was cared for and to fulfill my obligations to serve in the Church. I learned to curtail my activities so I could have strength for the most essential events and op-portunities. I had good doctors, and I was continually learning about my illness and how to reduce its effects.

I received numerous priesthood blessings, and my husband and I did the spiritual work of fasting and praying for help. We were always seeking answers and miracles. I knew that we did receive direction, but it seemed that there was never a genuine improvement in my health. I occasionally studied my patriarchal blessing, and I sensed from its prophecy that I would not have to endure a lifetime of sickness. I was always thinking about what I could do to effect a dramatic change to-ward good health.

One sleepless night I was bewildered by conflicting advice I had received. Needing peace and comfort while I arranged my thoughts, I determined to spend some formal time pondering solutions and ap-proaches. I yearned for direction and partnership with the Lord as I talked things over with myself. In my living room, I prayed for guid-ance, and then I wrote things I had been impressed to think about. I wrote what was on my mind and what I was feeling. I listed my bless-ings and all the things that were going well in my life and in our family. It was a long list. I wrote the things I knew I had received help with, and that was a long list. I wrote the questions I did not have answers to, and that was a long list. I then prioritized the things I needed to improve and learn more about.

Throughout that night, I felt a peaceful presence as I worked through my agenda. As I concluded my ponderings and said an-other prayer, I no longer felt overwhelmed. I had a clear idea of what I needed to do next in order to get well. I was able to leave worries behind and begin anew with a plan for my recovery. My recovery was not immediate, but from that night, I had clear direction and peace, and I was able to patiently do all I had been directed to do. I felt I had received revelation for my life—how to improve and move forward. I had been in darkness and confusion, but I was now filled with hope and faith.

From the experience of that night and many others times, I have learned that I can confidently approach the Lord for help. I have also learned that I need to be earnest and sincere in my desire for His guidance. As I have followed these principles, I have felt His help in formal approaches to Him, in simple prayers, in my heart, in meetings, in my car, while I walk. He has blessed me many times over. I have received direction for challenges our children have faced and in countless other dilemmas. I have a firm testimony that the spirit of revelation has been with me as I have qualified for it.

I have often taught that "the ability to qualify for, receive, and act on personal revelation is the single most important skill that can be acquired in this life."[1] A skill is something we learn about and then improve in until we become proficient at it. To develop the skill of receiving and acting on personal revelation, we need to learn what revelation feels like, what it is, and what is it not.

WHAT REVELATION IS

Revelation is two-way communication with God. The most important revelation we receive is a testimony of our Heavenly Father and His Son through the power of the Holy Ghost. The Holy Ghost can also guide us in our life experiences as we seek His help. Personal revelation comes to us when we "look unto God with firmness of mind, and pray unto him with exceeding faith."[2] We seek revelation because we know our Heavenly Father has a plan for us, His children, and because we know that this life is a preparation for the life to come.

THE CLIMATE FOR REVELATION

Revelation thrives in a climate that is conducive to the Holy Ghost—the Spirit. If we are living in chaos, if we offend the Spirit by our actions, if we insult the Spirit, we cannot expect to receive His revelatory help. We invite the Spirit by establishing a climate around us where He will feel welcome. When we repent and try to become more like the Lord, we are seeking His Spirit.

When Jesus Christ restored His gospel through Joseph Smith, some of His first revelations recorded by the Prophet included direction on personal revelation. In many of the first sections of the Doctrine and Covenants, we learn about the climate for revelation and about our responsibility to prepare to receive answers from the Lord. Just as many early Latter-day Saints were spiritually immature and did not understand how to seek, receive, and act on revelation, we are learning how to use this magnificent gift to communicate with the Lord. We can learn from His counsel to the early Saints:

"Repent and walk more uprightly before me, and . . . yield to the persuasions of men no more."[3]

"Keep my commandments, and seek to bring forth and establish the cause of Zion; seek not for riches but for wisdom, and behold, the mysteries of God shall be unfolded unto you."[4]

"Look unto me in every thought; doubt not, fear not."[5]

"Assuredly as the Lord liveth, who is your God and your Redeemer, even so surely shall you receive a knowledge of whatsoever things you shall ask in faith, with an honest heart, believing that you shall receive. . . . I will tell you in your mind and in your heart, by the Holy Ghost, which shall come upon you and which shall dwell in your heart. . . . Remember that without faith you can do nothing; therefore ask in faith."[6]

"You must study it out in your mind; then you must ask me if it be right."[7]

"Pray always, that you may come off conqueror."[8]

As followers of Christ, we need to develop the ability to hear the voice of the Lord through the Spirit. In order to receive revelation, we must do private work to keep our spiritual lives in condition and be ready to receive help when we ask for it.

RECOGNIZING THE VOICE OF THE LORD

Each of us has the responsibility and privilege to learn to recognize the voice of the Lord. This is a personal communication, and learning to respond to it is fundamental in our spiritual development. Part of recognizing His voice is recognizing its effects on us. The Apostle Paul described the product of help from the Holy Ghost: "The fruit of the Spirit is love, joy, peace, longsuffering, gentleness, goodness, faith, meekness, temperance."[9]

Elizabeth Ann Whitney, an early member of the Church, described what she felt after embracing the gospel and its laws: "A fresh revelation of the Spirit day by day, an unveiling of mysteries which before were dark, deep, unexplained and incomprehensible; a most implicit faith in a divine power, in infinite truth emanating from God the Father."[10]

As we learn to recognize the Lord's voice, we make better choices, prioritize our lives, take care of responsibilities, and develop ourselves more fully. The Lord said:

"Put your trust in that Spirit which leadeth to do good—yea, to do justly, to walk humbly, to judge righteously; and this is my Spirit.

"Verily, verily, I say unto you, I will impart unto you of my Spirit, which shall enlighten your mind, which shall fill your soul with joy;

"And then shall ye know, or by this shall you know, all things whatsoever you desire of me, which are pertaining unto things of righteousness, in faith believing in me that you shall receive."[11]

WHAT REVELATION IS NOT

When we know what the influence of the Lord's Spirit feels like, it is easier to determine what revelation is not. Revelation is not unhappy, contentious, selfish, or stubborn. It is not a stupor, and it is not uncertainty, timidity, doubt, or lack of confidence. It is not self-centered or prideful. It is not a hunch or a guess or a knee-jerk reaction. It is not blaming or shifting of responsibility to others. It is not a club or weapon to beat others with, because it is not manipulative or coercive. It is not a justification for poor choices. It is not squeezed or forced or time-bound.

WORKING TO RECEIVE PERSONAL REVELATION

The Lord sends His help in His way, in His time.[12] Revelation does not occur in a vacuum. For instance, if we have not studied the scriptures, we should not expect the Lord to bring those words to our remembrance. If we have not carefully learned about the nature of the problems we are trying to solve, we should not expect the Lord to provide support or enlightenment to make up for our lack of effort. It is much like going to school. We collect facts, consult with experts, and make sincere judgments and evaluations. When we study the best solutions, get the best advice available, and learn more about how to solve difficult problems, we are prepared to receive heavenly help.

The adversary is opportunistic. He can mimic or counterfeit many feelings and give false assurances. But he cannot duplicate the peace that comes through the Holy Ghost. The adversary enjoys creating confusion, commotion, contention. When we do the important work

121

to know what our best options are, we diminish the potential for his interference.

Elder Neal A. Maxwell taught that revelation does not consist "only of supernal events like the First Vision." He said that it is "usually a quiet, inward, but real and powerful process." It "requires serious mental effort on our part. We have to take real thought, and then we have to continue as we commenced (see D&C 9:5–11).... Revelation is not a matter of pushing buttons, but of pushing ourselves, often aided by fasting, scripture study, and personal pondering."[13]

AGENCY

We fought a war in heaven for the opportunity to make our own choices. This means that we must not leave all decisions up to the Lord. One of the great purposes of our lives is for us to learn how to be agents and to make choices for ourselves. The Lord has said, "It is not meet that I should command in all things."[14] He has given us the great gift to be agents unto ourselves.[15] He has given us brains so we can think, form opinions, and learn. We are to use our own experiences and talents to help us make decisions.

Elder Bruce R. McConkie taught:

"We're expected to use the gifts and talents and abilities, the sense and judgment and agency with which we are endowed.

"But on the other hand, we're commanded to seek the Lord, to desire his Spirit, to get the spirit of revelation and inspiration in our lives. We come unto the Church and a legal administrator places his hands upon our head and says, 'Receive the Holy Ghost.' This gives us the gift of the Holy Ghost, which is the right to the constant companionship of that member of the Godhead, based on faithfulness.

"And so we're faced with two propositions. One is that we ought to be guided by the spirit of inspiration, the spirit of revelation. The other is that we're here under a direction to use our agency, to determine what we ought to do on our own; and we need to strike a fine balance between these two, if we're going to pursue a course that will give us joy and satisfaction and peace in this life and lead to eternal reward in our Father's kingdom."[16]

THE RIGHT QUESTIONS

I have learned that asking the right questions is just as important as getting the right answers. The wrong questions rarely lead to the right answers. When we ponder deeply about our questions, we will be more likely to get the answers right. Many times, if we have the right question, the answer is obvious. And the right questions often lead us to receive revelation beyond the answers we think we are looking for. More often than not, the Lord waits for us to ask questions that will allow Him to teach us more about Himself and that will prepare us to develop spiritually so we can be more like Him.

Life is full of messy problems, and we often arrive at solutions and personal growth though arduous and untidy passages. Quick solutions rarely stretch us. We will grow stronger as we seek the right questions by pondering, evaluating, sifting and re-sifting, and listening and listening again.

WALKING BY FAITH

I have learned that the Lord is kind, interested, attentive, responsive, and patient. Sometimes He gives us answers speedily, in urgent moments of need. Sometimes He blesses us with feelings of caution and a sense that we should be deliberate and careful. He often waits to give us answers until we are ready for them, until we have grown a little more. In the Gospel of Mark, we read of disciples in ancient times who were with the Savior on the Sea of Galilee. The Savior instructed His disciples to get into a ship and go to the other side of the sea. He went away to a mountain to pray. Then a terrifying storm arose, tossing the disciples in their boat. We read: "And when even was come, the ship was in the midst of the sea, and he alone on the land. And he saw them toiling in rowing; for the wind was contrary unto them: and about the fourth watch of the night he cometh unto them, walking upon the sea, . . . and saith unto them, Be of good cheer: it is I; be not afraid."[17]

The Lord parted from His disciples before the evening, and through the long night He observed them striving against the storm. He did not go to them until just before dawn.[18] We learn from this account that our Lord often allows us to struggle with difficult challenges, through dark and frightening nights. He knows we need to develop spiritual muscle, courage, charity, and faith to become more like Him. He needs us to understand His nature and His power and His love for us. Sometimes it is only by looking backward that we see that we have been guided and instructed.

It is our blessing to have ongoing help from heaven. The Lord has said, "He that lacketh wisdom, let him ask of me, and I will give him liberally and upbraid him not."[19] He has promised, "If thou shalt ask, thou shalt receive revelation upon revelation, knowledge upon knowledge, that thou mayest know the mysteries and peaceable things—that which bringeth joy, that which bringeth life eternal."[20] Through revelation, we can know of "things as they really are, and of things as they really will be."[21]

This assurance enables us to continue to seek the companionship of the Spirit and trust in the Lord's counsel: "Be of good cheer, for I will lead you along."[22]

NOTES

1. Julie B. Beck, "And upon the Handmaids in Those Days Will I Pour Out My Spirit," *Ensign,* May 2010, 11; quoted in *Daughters in My Kingdom: The History and Work of Relief Society* (2011), 158.
2. Jacob 3:1.
3. Doctrine and Covenants 5:21.
4. Doctrine and Covenants 6:6–7.
5. Doctrine and Covenants 6:36.
6. Doctrine and Covenants 8:1–2, 10.
7. Doctrine and Covenants 9:8.
8. Doctrine and Covenants 10:5.
9. Galatians 5:22–23.
10. Elizabeth Ann Whitney, "A Leaf from an Autobiography," *Woman's Exponent,* Aug. 1, 1878, 33; quoted in *Daughters in My Kingdom,* 129.
11. Doctrine and Covenants 11:12–14.
12. See Jacob 4:10.
13. Neal A. Maxwell, "Revelation," First Worldwide Leadership Training Meeting, Jan. 11, 2003, 5.
14. Doctrine and Covenants 58:26.
15. See Doctrine and Covenants 58:28.
16. Bruce R. McConkie, "Agency or Inspiration—Which?" (devotional address at Brigham Young University, Feb 27, 1973), 2; speeches.byu.edu /wp-content/uploads/pdf/McConkie_Bruce_1973-02.pdf.
17. Mark 6:47–48, 50; see also verses 45–46, 49.
18. See Bible Dictionary, "Watches," 788.
19. Doctrine and Covenants 42:68; see also James 1:5–6.
20. Doctrine and Covenants 42:61.
21. Jacob 4:13.
22. Doctrine and Covenants 78:18.

12

WHY WE ARE ORGANIZED INTO QUORUMS AND RELIEF SOCIETIES

At the time of my call as Relief Society General President in 2007, I had been serving in the Young Women organization for nearly a decade. I needed to know more about Relief Society, so I started studying. It was not long before I discovered a truth that the Prophet Joseph Smith taught. The Relief Society, he said, was a restoration of an ancient pattern. This truth led me to search for that pattern and better understand the Lord's invitation to women to labor with Him. For the next four and a half years, I searched the words of prophets about Relief Society and also about Melchizedek Priesthood quorums and their parallel work. From the fat folders of talks and information I collected, I prepared what I call my "thesis" about the essential work of the men and women in the restored Church of Jesus Christ. I presented this message at a Brigham Young University devotional on January 17, 2012.

In the April 2018 general conference, the Lord inspired prophets, seers, and revelators to make significant adjustments to the way Melchizedek Priesthood quorums are organized. He also inspired them to replace home teaching and visiting teaching with an effort called ministering, with a focus on watchcare of individuals. As I reviewed the reflections in this chapter with the newly announced adjustments in mind, I found only a few places where I needed to alter my language. Prophets, seers, and revelators have always taught principles of leadership, and care for individuals has always been their priority.

⁓

When my father was called to preside over the Brazilian Mission, there was only a single mission in Brazil. I was four at the time. There were no stakes or wards; there wasn't an elders quorum in the country. That means there were no home teachers. There were over forty branches, which were generally presided over by missionaries who conducted a weekly sacrament meeting and sometimes held Sunday School and branch activities. My father had served as a stake president and a bishop prior to his call as a mission president, and he had an understanding of how to establish the Lord's Church. He began to organize branches and districts in the pattern we are familiar with today in anticipation of future stakes and wards.

To begin the organization, some priorities were followed. First, a branch president and then an elders quorum president and a Relief Society president were called. It was understood that there could be no functioning branch without a quorum president and a Relief Society president.

As the Prophet Joseph Smith began establishing the Church in this dispensation, the Lord directed him to follow similar inspired patterns. When he set the course for the Relief Society, he told the sisters they were organized "under the priesthood after the pattern of the priesthood."[1] This gave the sisters official responsibilities in the restored Church and the authority to function in those responsibilities. This was a pattern similar to that given to a president of a quorum of elders, who was to counsel with his presidency.[2]

Before we can understand why we are thus organized, it may be helpful to review the definition of a priesthood quorum and a Relief

Society. Many people have the mistaken idea that a quorum or a Relief Society is merely a class or a place to sit during the third hour of church on Sunday. Perhaps some of this misunderstanding started to develop when the Church combined its major meetings into a three-hour block on Sunday. Before that time, quorum and Relief Society meetings were not connected with sacrament meeting or Sunday School.

Membership in a quorum has been called "a steady, sustaining citizenship."[3] President Boyd K. Packer has said that quorums are "selected assemblies of brethren given authority that [the Lord's] business might be transacted and His work proceed."[4] He also said that "in ancient days when a man was appointed to a select body, his commission, always written in Latin, outlined the responsibility of the organization, defined who should be members, and then invariably contained the words: *quorum vos unum* meaning, 'of whom we will that you be one.'"[5]

President Spencer W. Kimball taught that "the Relief Society is the Lord's organization for women. It complements the priesthood training given to the brethren."[6] The word *society* has a meaning nearly identical to that of *quorum*. It connotes "an enduring and co-operating . . . group" distinguished by its common aims and beliefs.[7] When Joseph Smith organized the sisters, he told them that "there should be a select society, separate from all the evils of the world, choice, virtuous, and holy."[8] President Joseph F. Smith taught that Relief Society has its own unique identity and that it was "divinely made, divinely authorized, divinely instituted, divinely ordained of God to minister for the salvation of the souls of women and of men."[9]

The purposes of Relief Society are to increase faith and personal righteousness, strengthen families and homes, and seek out and provide relief for those who are in need.[10] The quorum is to serve others, build unity and brotherhood, instruct quorum members in the doctrines and principles of the gospel, and watch over the Church.[11]

Being part of a Relief Society or quorum is a designation for a way of life. We are to serve in the association of a Melchizedek Priesthood quorum or a Relief Society for a lifetime. From the quorum or Relief Society, we are called to serve in other Church assignments and organizations, such as missionary work, temple service, Sunday School, seminary or institute, Young Men, Primary, Young Women, and so forth. No matter where we serve, we always retain our "citizenship" in and our responsibility to the quorum or Relief Society. President Packer has taught that all service in the Church strengthens the higher priesthood and Relief Society and is a demonstration of our devotion to Relief Society and quorum membership.[12]

It is true that each of us is responsible for becoming a faithful, covenant-keeping disciple of the Lord Jesus Christ. Some may argue that we can accomplish this as individuals without the benefit of a supporting group. But President David O. McKay said that if priesthood men only needed "personal distinction or individual elevation, there would be no need of groups or quorums. The very existence of such groups, established by divine authorization, proclaims our dependence upon one another, the indispensable need of mutual help and assistance."[13]

Inasmuch as the Lord chose to organize us in this way, it is important for us to seek for a greater understanding as to why we are thus organized and then to seek to fulfill the vision He has for us. To help facilitate that understanding I have drawn heavily from the scriptures and words of prophets to illustrate, only briefly, five important reasons why we are organized into quorums and Relief Societies.

One of the reasons we have quorums and Relief Societies is to organize us under the priesthood and after the pattern of the priesthood.[14] Our God is a God of order, and all that He does to build His kingdom is done through His priesthood patterns.

One of those patterns is the organization of wards and stakes, each with a geographic boundary. Each ward is guided by a bishop who holds the keys, or the Lord's authority, for his ward. He is the shepherd of the Lord's flock within his ward and has the charge to see to the temporal and spiritual needs of that flock. Only he can authorize the ordinances that are essential for the salvation of the members of that flock. His responsibility is monumental and is the more difficult because he is only one man who cannot possibly watch over all of the sheep at once. The quorum and Relief Society leaders are seen by the bishop as undershepherds who magnify, enhance, and distribute his watchcare.

The formation of a presidency is also a priesthood pattern. Every ward elders quorum president and Relief Society president presides over and directs the activities of the elders quorum or Relief Society in the ward.[15] Quorum and Relief Society leaders have a measure of divine authority given to them regarding the government and instruction of those they are called to lead.[16] They are men and women who are "called of God, by prophecy, and by the laying on of hands."[17] To preside means to stand guard, to superintend, and to lead.[18] This means that Relief Society and quorum leaders in a ward carry the responsibility to supervise, oversee, and regulate the work of the Relief Society and the quorums on behalf of the bishop.

Sustaining those who are called to lead is also a priesthood pattern. We do not select our leaders by popular vote, as is common in organizations outside the Church. It is an act of our faith in the Lord and those who are called to lead in His Church to sustain their actions and support them in their responsibilities to lead us. When Joseph

Smith organized the Relief Society, he "exhorted the sisters always to concentrate their faith and prayers for, and place confidence in those whom God has appointed to honor, whom God has placed at the head to lead."[19]

One of the priesthood patterns we enjoy is the ability to receive revelation. When Joseph Smith organized the Relief Society, he said the sisters were "to get instruction through the order which God has established—through the medium of those appointed to lead."[20] This ability and promise regarding personal revelation is one of the remarkable blessings that come to every quorum and Relief Society presidency. When the Lord said that each of us was to learn our duty and act in the office to which we are appointed,[21] He provided a way for us to do just that. I have seen humble Relief Society and quorum presidencies in many parts of the world leading with great and inspiring ability because they are organized under the priesthood and after the order of the priesthood. They follow patterns that allow them to get revelation for the work they have been set apart to do.

At the time of the Relief Society centennial, the First Presidency wrote: "We ask our Sisters of the Relief Society never to forget that they are a unique organization in the whole world, for they were organized under the inspiration of the Lord. . . . No other woman's organization in all the earth has had such a birth."[22]

A second reason we are organized into quorums and Relief Societies is to focus Heavenly Father's sons and daughters on the work of salvation and to engage them in it. Quorums and Relief Societies are an organized discipleship with the responsibility to assist in our Father's work to bring about eternal life for His children. We are not in the entertainment business; we are in the salvation business. Entrance into an elders quorum or a Relief Society usually follows a significant investment from the Lord and His leaders in the teaching and preparation of younger members of the Church for such a work. The work of salvation includes missionary work and retaining in activity those who are converted. We are to do all we can to bring back into activity those of our group who have weakened in their faith. The work of a quorum and a Relief Society also focuses on temple and family history work. We carry the responsibility to teach the gospel and exemplify righteous living to one another.

The work of salvation also includes improving our temporal and spiritual self-reliance. And as a group we ensure that the needy and the poor are cared for. Elder John A. Widtsoe defined the saving work of the Relief Society as the "relief of poverty, relief of illness; relief of doubt, relief of ignorance—relief of all that hinders the joy and progress of woman."[23] These same kinds of responsibilities are given to a quorum. They are honorable and heavy responsibilities. They connote a sacred trust and imply a significant contribution to the Lord's work of salvation—a work that is both a burden and a blessing. When quorums and Relief Societies are unified in this work, they each essentially take an oar in the boat—each helping move us toward salvation.

When we are organized into Relief Societies and quorums, our personal discipleship is extended and we become engaged with others in the saving work that was modeled by the Savior. It is never modest or inconsequential. It forces us to a higher path of discipleship and a greater spiritual maturity. It is often a long-suffering and patient work and can seem thankless because there is usually a noticeable absence of public recognition for the good we do. Elder Widtsoe taught that "to save souls opens the whole field of human activity and development."[24] The work of salvation is guided by the Spirit, who confirms our actions, assures us of the Lord's approval, and supplies the true joy that comes with an affirmation of our success.

A third reason we are organized into quorums and Relief

Societies is to help bishops wisely manage the Lord's storehouse. The Lord's storehouse includes the "time, talents, compassion, materials, and financial means"[25] of the members of the Church. The talents of the Saints are to be used to help care for the poor and the needy and to build the Lord's kingdom. The Lord envisions "every man seeking the interest of his neighbor, and doing all things with an eye single to the glory of God."[26]

Bishops have charge of the Lord's storehouse, and they depend on the quorums and Relief Societies to help them seek out and care for all in their wards. Every ward is unique and can be said to have its own DNA. This makes it essential that the leaders of the quorums and Relief Societies work in councils to help bishops manage and apportion the Lord's assets. Together they evaluate the strengths and abilities of individuals and ensure that the Lord's sheep are cared for.

Our Savior taught this principle in many ways during His mortal ministry, and the scriptures contain many examples of how He looked after those who were in need. In every ward there are always a few dedicated souls who would do all of the work while others would neglect their duty and fail to offer their gifts. Quorum and Relief Society leaders have the responsibility to organize and carry out an inspired ministry to help all brothers and sisters keep their covenants to remember the Savior and consecrate their lives to His work.

If we were left to ourselves, we might prefer to care only for the popular, charming, and grateful people in our wards. It is much more challenging to care for those who are difficult to love, who have grave and complicated challenges, or who do not seem to appreciate our help. The Savior said:

"Love your enemies, bless them that curse you, do good to them that hate you, and pray for them which despitefully use you, and persecute you;

"That ye may be the children of your Father which is in heaven: for he maketh his sun to rise on the evil and on the good, and sendeth rain on the just and on the unjust.

"For if ye love them which love you, what reward have ye? do not even the publicans the same?

"And if ye salute your brethren only, what do ye more than others? do not even the publicans so?[27]

"Ye are therefore commanded to be perfect, even as your Father who is in heaven is perfect."[28]

One of the most significant ways this kind of watchcare is apportioned is through ministering. President Henry B. Eyring said, "The only system [that can] provide succor and comfort across a church so large in a world so varied would be through individual servants near the people in need."[29] Elder Bruce R. McConkie, who served faithfully as an Apostle of the Lord Jesus Christ, called an elder "a shepherd serving in the sheepfold of the Good Shepherd." When they serve as ministering brothers, they are "sent by their quorum president, by the bishop, and by the Lord."[30]

President Thomas S. Monson taught, "Modern revelation commission[s] those ordained to the priesthood to 'teach, expound, exhort, baptize, and watch over the church ... and visit the house of each member, and exhort them to pray vocally and in secret and attend to all family duties, ... to watch over the church always, and be with and strengthen them; and see that there is no iniquity in the church, neither hardness with each other, neither lying, backbiting, nor evil speaking' (Doctrine and Covenants 20:42, 47, 53–54). . . .

"From the Book of Mormon, Alma 'consecrated all their priests and all their teachers; and none were consecrated except they were just men. Therefore they did watch over their people, and did nourish them with things pertaining to righteousness' (Mosiah 23:17–18). . . .

"We are wise if we learn and understand the challenges of the members of each family."[31]

President Henry B. Eyring told the sisters to consider an assignment to minister "as a call from the Lord."[32] President Kimball said to the sisters, "Your duties in many ways must be much like those of the [elders], which briefly are 'to watch over the church always'—not twenty minutes a month but always."[33]

Ministering becomes the Lord's work when our focus is centered on people rather than on percentages. The perfection of our statistics is not a good measure of our watchcare. We can never say that we are done ministering. When we represent the Lord we are always on His errand. President Thomas S. Monson taught, "Ours is the responsibility to teach, to inspire, to motivate, to bring to activity and to eventual exaltation the sons and daughters of God."[34] When we give an account of our stewardship, we are to report the spiritual and temporal well-being of those we are assigned to care for. We can also report any service we render. Special or urgent needs should always be reported immediately.[35] The only true measures of our success in this effort are the confirmations of the Spirit for our efforts and when those we are assigned to watch over can say three important things:

1. "She (or he) helps me grow spiritually."
2. "I know she (or he) cares deeply about me and my family."
3. "If I have problems, I know she (or he) will take action without waiting to be invited."

The Lord said, "And if any man among you be strong in the Spirit, let him take with him him that is weak, that he may be edified in all meekness, that he may become strong also."[36] When these measures are our aim, then we organize and function in an inspired rather than a programmatic way.

A fourth reason for why we are organized into quorums and Relief Societies is to provide a defense and a refuge for Heavenly Father's children and their families in the latter days. President Thomas S. Monson has said: "Today, we are encamped against the greatest array of sin, vice, and evil ever assembled before our eyes. . . . The battle plan whereby we fight to save the souls of men is not our own."[37]

We are all in the midst of a mortal experience. We all chose this experience, and the Lord will ensure that we all have one. An age-old anti-Christ deception implies that people who are smart enough or rich enough can avoid challenges.[38] This is not so! In our lives and the world today we are experiencing in full measure the "perilous times"[39] of the last days the Apostle Paul described to Timothy. As our times become ever more difficult, the faithful brothers and sisters in quorums and Relief Societies are to protect the homes of Zion from the shrill voices of the world and the provocative influence of the adversary.

We have been taught by President Dallin H. Oaks that "one of the great functions of Relief Society is to provide sisterhood for women, just as priesthood quorums provide brotherhood for men."[40] It is our blessing to be part of a sisterhood or a brotherhood that provides "a place of healing, love, kindness, care, and belonging."[41] President Packer said: "This great circle of sisters will be a protection for each of you and for your families. The Relief Society might be likened to a refuge. . . . You will be safe within it. It encircles each sister like a protecting wall."[42] He said: "How consoling it is to know that no matter where [a family may] go, a Church family awaits them. From the day they arrive, he will belong to a quorum of the priesthood and she will belong to Relief Society."[43]

Elder D. Todd Christofferson recounted the story of Brother

George Goates, who in six days lost his son Charles and three of Charles's small children during the flu epidemic of 1918. That week Brother Goates made the caskets, dug the graves, and helped prepare the burial clothing. His child and grandchildren died during the week he was to harvest his sugar beet crop, which was left freezing in the ground. After the burials, he and another son went to their fields to see if they could salvage any of their crop. When they arrived, they saw the members of his quorum leaving the empty field. His quorum had harvested every sugar beet. It was then that this man who had shown tremendous strength in the previous week sat down and sobbed like a child. He looked up to the sky and said, "Thanks, Father, for the elders of our ward."[44]

Whatever our mortal experience, we can have this feeling of fellowship and have the support and strength of many around us. The Lord said, "Also the body hath need of every member, that all may be edified together, that the system may be kept perfect."[45] In the sisterhood of Relief Society and the brotherhood of the quorums, we can find refuge and protection from the storms of life and the calamities of the latter days.

A fifth purpose for being organized into quorums and Relief Societies is to strengthen and support us in our family roles and responsibilities as sons and daughters of God. Though many of our responsibilities in the Church are parallel, Heavenly Father's sons and daughters each have unique and distinct responsibilities in the family and in the Church. Quorums and Relief Societies are to teach our Heavenly Father's sons and daughters and inspire them to prepare for the blessings of eternal life. Our Father sees the potential of His sons and His daughters to be family leaders. Therefore, everything we do in quorums and Relief Societies is to help the Lord with His mission of preparing His children for the blessings of the eternal life He envisions for us. In these settings we are meant to learn how to become part of our Heavenly Father's eternal family.

The quorum and the Relief Society assist family leaders and future family leaders and help them establish patterns and practices of righteous behavior and covenant keeping in their lives. Brothers and sisters encourage one another to pray always, pay tithes and offerings, and renew covenants on the Lord's holy day. They are to help one another be sufficiently mature to make and keep sacred temple covenants.

The quorum and the Relief Society should help us become who our Heavenly Father needs us to become. Joseph Smith taught the sisters from 1 Corinthians about the importance of developing godlike qualities. He said the sisters were organized "according to [their] natures" and were "placed in a situation in which [they could] act according to those sympathies which God has planted in [them]."[46] It is for this reason that the motto of Relief Society, "Charity never faileth," was chosen.

Sister Eliza R. Snow, second Relief Society General President, said to the sisters: "We want to be ladies in very deed, not according to the term of the word as the world judges, but fit companions of the Gods and Holy Ones. In an organized capacity we can assist each other in not only doing good but in refining ourselves, and whether few or many come forward and help to prosecute this great work, they will be those that will fill honorable positions in the Kingdom of God. . . . Women should be women and not babies that need petting and correction all the time. I know we like to be appreciated, but if we do not get all the appreciation which we think is our due, what matters?"[47]

It is in the quorum that brothers are taught to "rise up" as "men of God" and "have done with lesser things. / Give heart and soul and mind and strength / To serve the King of Kings."[48] The work of the quorum and the Relief Society clarifies the unique identities and responsibilities of sons and daughters of God and unifies them in defense of His plan. President Harold B. Lee stated:

"It seems clear to me that the Church has *no choice*—and never has had—but to do more to assist the *family* in carrying out *its* divine mission, not only because that is the order of heaven, but also because that is the most *practical* contribution we can make to our youth—to help improve the quality of life in the Latter-day Saint homes. As important as our many programs and organizational efforts are, these *should not* supplant the home; they should *support* the home."[49]

As the Lord said to Emma Smith, we are to "lay aside the things of this world, and seek for the things of a better. . . . Cleave unto the covenants which thou hast made. . . . Keep my commandments continually, and a crown of righteousness thou shalt receive."[50] Each of us is a beloved daughter or son of God with sacred personal responsibilities. In our quorums and Relief Societies we are to be taught and inspired to become who our Father in Heaven created us to become.

OUR RESPONSIBILITY AND PROMISE

There is much work a quorum must do as a quorum and much a Relief Society is to do as a circle of sisters, and there is much that is to be coordinated between them. Because "the Lord's Church is governed through councils,"[51] it is important for the Relief Society president to be included in meetings in which confidential welfare matters are discussed and in which bishops can facilitate the coordination of ministering brothers and sisters.[52]

President Gordon B. Hinckley said:

"It will be a marvelous day, my brethren . . . when our priesthood quorums become an anchor of strength to every man belonging thereto, when each such man may appropriately be able to say, 'I am a member of a priesthood quorum of The Church of Jesus Christ of Latter-day Saints. I stand ready to assist my brethren in all of their needs, as I am confident they stand ready to assist me in mine. Working together, we shall grow spiritually as covenant sons of God. Working together, we can stand, without embarrassment and without fear, against every wind of adversity that might blow, be it economic, social, or spiritual.'"[53]

President Packer recently declared to the brethren of the Church: "We need everyone. The tired or worn out or lazy and even those who are bound down with guilt. . . . Too many of our priesthood brethren are living below their privileges and the Lord's expectations."[54] "In one of the first meetings of the Female Relief Society of Nauvoo, Joseph Smith admonished the sisters to 'live up to [their] privilege.'"[55] In a similar vein, President Packer said to the sisters of Relief Society: "Rally to the cause of Relief Society! Strengthen it! Attend it! Devote yourselves to it! Enlist the inactive in it and bring nonmember sisters under the influence of it. It is time now to unite in this worldwide circle of sisters. A strong, well-organized Relief Society is crucial to the future, to the safety of this Church."[56]

Many of the principles in this chapter can be found in *Daughters in My Kingdom: The History and Work of Relief Society.* This resource from the First Presidency can help brothers and sisters learn how to fulfill their responsibilities. Through this and other instructions, we "know how to act and direct [the] church, how to act upon the points of [the Lord's] law and commandments, which [He has] given." We are now to "bind [ourselves] to act in all holiness before [Him]."[57]

What the Lord envisioned regarding quorums and Relief Societies has not yet been fully utilized. Many quorums and Relief Societies are at present much like sleeping giants waiting for you to breathe new life into them.

The true restored gospel of Jesus Christ is upon the earth. My testimony of that restoration has been strengthened by knowing that quorums and Relief Societies were established so the Lord could organize His sons and daughters under the priesthood and after the pattern of the priesthood. By this means He engages His children in His work of salvation and in wisely managing His storehouse. Quorums and Relief Societies are meant to be a safety and a refuge in these difficult days and to support and strengthen the identity, roles, and responsibilities of Heavenly Father's sons and daughters. We are "called by the voice of the Prophet of God to do it,"[58] and, as we do so, "the angels cannot be restrained from being [our] associates."[59]

Author's note: Please refer to speeches from the April 2018 general conference for more information regarding the work of quorums and Relief Societies.

NOTES

1. Joseph Smith, quoted in Sarah M. Kimball, "Auto-Biography," *Woman's Exponent* 12, no. 7 (1 September 1883): 51; cited in *Daughters in My Kingdom: The History and Work of Relief Society* (2011), 12.
2. See Doctrine and Covenants 107:21.
3. Boyd K. Packer, "What Every Elder Should Know—and Every Sister as Well: A Primer on Principles of Priesthood Government," *Ensign*, February 1993, 9.
4. Boyd K. Packer, "What Every Elder Should Know," *Ensign*, February 1993, 9.
5. Boyd K. Packer, in "Supplemental Readings, Section B," *A Royal Priesthood*, Melchizedek Priesthood study guide, 1975–76 (1975), 131.
6. Spencer W. Kimball, "First Presidency Message: Relief Society—Its Promise and Potential," *Ensign*, March 1976, 4; quoted in *Teachings of Presidents of the Church: Spencer W. Kimball* (2006), 217.
7. *Merriam-Webster's Collegiate Dictionary*, 11th ed. (2003), s.v. "society," 1184.

8. Joseph Smith, in Relief Society Minute Book, Nauvoo, Illinois, 30 March 1842, 22; spelling, punctuation, and capitalization standardized as needed in all excerpts from this minute book; quoted in *Daughters in My Kingdom,* 15.

9. Joseph F. Smith, in Minutes of the General Board of Relief Society, 17 March 1914, Church History Library, 54–55; quoted in *Daughters in My Kingdom,* 66.

10. See *Handbook 2: Administering the Church* (2010), 9.1.1, 9.4.1; available at http://lds.org/bc/content/shared/content/english/pdf/language-materials/08702_eng.pdf?lang=eng; accessed 3 May 2018.

11. See *Handbook 2,* 7.1, 7.1.2; 8.1, 8.1.2; available at http://lds.org/bc/content/shared/content/english/pdf/language-materials/08702_eng.pdf?lang=eng; accessed 3 May 2018.

12. See Boyd K. Packer, "The Circle of Sisters," *Ensign,* November 1980, 110.

13. David O. McKay, in Conference Report, October 1968, 84.

14. See *Daughters in My Kingdom,* 12.

15. See Dallin H. Oaks, "The Relief Society and the Church," *Ensign,* May 1992, 35.

16. See Joseph Fielding Smith, "The Relief Society Organized by Revelation," *Relief Society Magazine,* January 1965, 5.

17. Articles of Faith 1:5.

18. See "preside," http://dictionary.reference.com/browse/preside.

19. Relief Society Minute Book, Nauvoo, Illinois, 28 April 1842, 37; available at http://www.josephsmithpapers.org/paper-summary/nauvoo-relief-society-minute-book/34; accessed 3 May 2018.

20. Joseph Smith, Relief Society Minute Book, Nauvoo, Illinois, 28 April 1842, 40; available at http://www.josephsmithpapers.org/paper-summary/nauvoo-relief-society-minute-book/37; accessed 3 May 2018; quoted in *Daughters in My Kingdom,* 14.

21. See Doctrine and Covenants 107:99.

22. First Presidency message, 3 July 1942, "To the Presidency, Officers and Members of the Relief Society," in *A Centenary of Relief Society, 1842–1942* (1942), 7; quoted in Boyd K. Packer, "The Circle of Sisters," 111.

23. John A. Widtsoe, *Evidences and Reconciliations,* arr. G. Homer Durham (1987), 308.

24. John A. Widtsoe, *Evidences and Reconciliations,* 308.

25. *Handbook 2,* 6.1.3; available at http://lds.org/bc/content/shared /content/english/pdf/language-materials/08702_eng.pdf?lang=eng; accessed 3 May 2018.

26. Doctrine and Covenants 82:19.

27. Matthew 5:44–47.

28. JST, Matthew 5:50.

29. Henry B. Eyring, "The Enduring Legacy of Relief Society," *Ensign,* November 2009, 123.

30. Bruce R. McConkie, "Speaking Today: Only an Elder," *Ensign,* June 1975, 66, 68.

31. Thomas S. Monson, "Home Teaching," 46–47; quoted in *Teachings of Thomas S. Monson* (2011), 139.

32. Henry B. Eyring, "The Enduring Legacy of Relief Society," *Ensign,* November 2009, 123.

33. Spencer W. Kimball, "A Vision of Visiting Teaching," *Ensign,* June 1978, 24; see also Doctrine and Covenants 20:53; quoted in *Daughters in My Kingdom,* 113.

34. Thomas S. Monson, "Prophets Speak—The Wise Obey," general conference leadership session, Friday, 3 April 1987; quoted in *Teachings of Thomas S. Monson,* 140.

35. See *Handbook 2,* 9.5–9.5.4; http://lds.org/bc/content/shared/content /english/pdf/language-materials/08702_eng.pdf?lang=eng.

36. Doctrine and Covenants 84:106.

37. Thomas S. Monson, "Correlation Brings Blessings," *Relief Society Magazine,* April 1967, 247.

38. See Alma 30:17.

39. 2 Timothy 3:1.

40. Dallin H. Oaks, "The Relief Society and the Church," *Ensign,* May 1992, 37.

41. *Daughters in My Kingdom,* 86.

42. Boyd K. Packer, "The Circle of Sisters," *Ensign,* November 1980, 110; quoted in *Daughters in My Kingdom,* 86.

43. Boyd K. Packer, "The Relief Society," *Ensign,* May 1998, 74; quoted in *Daughters in My Kingdom,* 87.

44. See D. Todd Christofferson, "The Priesthood Quorum," *Ensign,* November 1998, 40–41, quoting from Vaughn J. Featherstone, in

Conference Report, April 1973, 46–48; or "Now Abideth Faith, Hope, and Charity," *Ensign*, July 1973, 36–37.

45. Doctrine and Covenants 84:110.
46. Joseph Smith, in "History, 1838–1856, volume C-1 Addenda, 40; available at http://www.josephsmithpapers.org/paper-summary/history-1838-1856-volume-c-1-addenda/40; accessed 3 May 2018.
47. Eliza R. Snow, address to Lehi Ward Relief Society, 27 October 1869, Lehi Ward, Alpine (Utah) Stake, in Relief Society, Minute Book, 1868–79, Church History Library, Salt Lake City, 26–27.
48. "Rise Up, O Men of God," *Hymns of The Church of Jesus Christ of Latter-day Saints* (1985), no. 323.
49. Harold B. Lee, "Message from the First Presidency: Preparing Our Youth," *Ensign*, March 1971, 3; emphasis added.
50. Doctrine and Covenants 25:10, 13, 15.
51. *Handbook 2*, 4.1; http://lds.org/bc/content/shared/content/english/pdf/language-materials/08702_eng.pdf?lang=eng.
52. See *Handbook 2*, 4.3; http://lds.org/bc/content/shared/content/english/pdf/language-materials/08702_eng.pdf?lang=eng.
53. Gordon B. Hinckley, "Welfare Responsibilities of the Priesthood Quorums," *Ensign*, November 1977, 86.
54. Boyd K. Packer, "The Power of the Priesthood," *Ensign*, May 2010, 9.
55. *Daughters in My Kingdom*, 169, 171, quoting Joseph Smith, in Relief Society Minute Book, Nauvoo, Illinois, 28 April 1842, Church History Library, 38.
56. Boyd K. Packer, "The Circle of Sisters," *Ensign*, November 1980, 111.
57. Doctrine and Covenants 43:8, 9.
58. See Joseph F. Smith, in Minutes of the General Board of Relief Society, 17 March 1914, Church History Library, 54–55; quoted in *Daughters in My Kingdom*, 180.
59. See Joseph Smith, in Relief Society Minute Book, Nauvoo, Illinois, Apr. 28, 1842, 38–39; quoted in *Daughters in My Kingdom*, 181.

13

"LET MY LIFE BE MUSIC"

On my grandmother's piano in my family room sits a weathered set of volumes of classical and popular music from the early 1900s. My mother told me that her father found them in an old, almost-forgotten trunk. He rescued the books because he remembered his mother buying them from a peddler who stopped by their Wyoming ranch. He knew that in those days, his family did not have money to buy much of anything, and so the books must have been important to his mother even though his family had no instrument and no one in the home who read music. For years, my great-grandmother displayed the books on a homemade wooden shelf in their cabin. Although she left no record of why she bought the books, to me they are a symbol of her dreams, of something refined and important. I wonder how many times she dusted them and what she thought about as she did so. She was the daughter of early pioneers who left nearly everything they owned as they formed part of the exodus from Nauvoo. Although she did not see the fulfillment of all her dreams, many of them were realized in her posterity after she passed away. At a devotional at LDS Business College on February 12, 2013, I reflected on the sacrifices my ancestors made to keep their covenants and on the blessings I enjoy as a result.

My grandmother Duella Eyre Hamblin grew up on a ranch in the Bridger Valley of Wyoming. In that cold, windy place near the Mormon Pioneer Trail, Grandmother Duella expanded her natural gift for music by teaching herself to play the piano, and in Lyman, Wyoming, she sang with friends and played the piano for Church events.

GRANDMA'S SACRIFICE AND SERVICE

Grandma had a marvelous contralto voice, and, desiring to improve her musical talents as a young adult, she moved to Salt Lake City to learn from a great music professor. This was an unusual music education for the time. In the approximately two years she lived in Salt Lake City, she sang with the Mormon Tabernacle Choir and studied at LDS Business College.

When she moved back to Wyoming, she and a young man named Marcene Hamblin, who also grew up in the Bridger Valley, fell in love. They were sealed in the Salt Lake Temple, and they moved to Murray, Utah. There Grandma began again to serve through music. She was the organist and accompanist in her ward. She served in that capacity for over 60 years, and she also sang in and organized choirs and groups to sing for graduations, celebrations, funerals, and hundreds of parties, thus bringing the gift of music into the lives of many, many people.

My grandparents' home was never without music. The first piece of furniture they acquired was a piano, purchased with the winnings from sporting events Grandpa had competed in. It was the central feature in their living room and was played every day. Grandpa was the son of my great-grandmother who had bought the music books from a peddler, and though he was never able to carry a tune, he delighted in the atmosphere of musical joy as Grandma and their children sang together and whistled through their tasks.

Grandma's motto was "Let my life be music." She displayed it in her kitchen, and it reflected her passion and vocation. She made great sacrifices to learn and share music. Because she understood the power of music, she wanted it in her family's life. She and Grandpa endured World War I and World War II and reared their family during the Great Depression. They always had limited financial means, but they always made room for music.

A BLESSING PASSED TO MY CHILDHOOD HOME

When my mother, the older of Grandma Duella's two daughters, was in the second grade, her teacher announced that if the children had any musical instrument at home, she would teach them to play it. Mother remembered seeing an old cornet under a bed, so she took that to school. In a short time, she was able to play it. She later bought a beautiful silver trumpet and eventually earned the first chair in the All-State High School Band and played with the University of Utah band.

I remember my mother, as the mission president's wife in Brazil, playing "To the Colors" and "Taps" for the raising and lowering of the flag on American holidays. She played beautiful and technically difficult solos for programs with the missionaries. She was still playing her trumpet for "breathing exercise" when she was over 90 years old.

My mother's love of music began when she was a little girl because of the influence of her mother. Because of this, she and my father provided the opportunity for all their children to learn to play the piano and other instruments. As a child, I did not realize the sacrifices and effort required to provide music lessons for 10 children. For me, it was just part of what we did as a family.

SHARING THE BLESSING WITH OUR
CHILDREN AND GRANDCHILDREN

Then came the time when my husband and I had the chance to give our own children music lessons. We had a little more money, a little more time, a little more prosperity than Grandma and Grandpa Hamblin had when they were raising their children. I had inherited my grandmother's piano, and that was what our children played, but a friend who was a national distributor for a piano company said, "I want you to have a grand piano." We saved our money until we could buy one, and then our children had two pianos to play, becoming experienced and gifted musicians. That skill enabled them to teach piano through high school and college, and they were blessed to graduate with no debt because of their ability to teach piano.

When our children were growing up, piano practice started very early in the morning on both pianos. They practiced up to three hours a day. Our children sometimes called it "combat piano." It wasn't just practicing—it was a required daily chore. On days when one or more of them didn't want to practice, I would sit with them to help them be more efficient with their time. I sat with one daughter almost every day for eight years because I knew she had a gift, but she didn't enjoy the work. One morning she said, "You can go do something else while I practice today. I actually like it now." Now she is a wonderful piano teacher because she has a great deal of empathy for her students and remembers how challenging it is to keep practicing when you don't really want to do the work.

Those times when I would think that I couldn't make the effort anymore or that it was too expensive or that it required too much sacrifice, I would remember the price my grandmother paid so that we could have this opportunity. I would think, "When I meet her again, what will her response to me be if I say, 'It was too hard'? How can I make that excuse to her?"

To keep us motivated during those years of long practice sessions and relentless preparation, I kept portraits of my Hamblin grandparents on our piano. Those pictures served as a reminder that in our generation we had a convergence of gifts and the opportunity to study music. I knew that someday we would be answerable to them for how we used the blessings they had passed to us. When we thought of Grandma and Grandpa and their sacrifices, our efforts became more consecrated.

We came to realize that piano was a vehicle to teach many life lessons. Through our music study, we learned about taking personal responsibility for individual preparation. We learned that lack of preparation is difficult to hide. We learned about partitioning large, nearly impossible tasks into smaller, more accessible goals. We learned about self-discipline and honesty. We acquired thinking and problem-solving skills. We learned about winning and losing and being good sports in both cases. The bonus was that our children also developed a marvelous talent they could share, and we all gained an appreciation for good music.

Now our grandchildren come to our home and practice on our pianos. My grandmother had no idea what she was beginning when she left her Wyoming valley. But she started an inspiring pattern that has now carried on through generations. Many of my siblings also have musical homes. Their children play instruments and sing. They have studied music, and music has enriched their lives. When I think of my grandmother's motto, "Let my life be music," I see her influence, in her children and on down to her great-great-grandchildren.

Through my grandmother's love of music, we learned a spiritual principle that applies in other areas of our lives—in our spiritual growth and our personal development. We learned that there is no easy road to God's greatest blessings, no shortcut to true happiness. The Lord teaches this in the Doctrine and Covenants:

"Ye cannot behold with your natural eyes, for the present time, the design of your God concerning those things which shall come hereafter, and the glory which shall follow after much tribulation.

"For after much tribulation come the blessings."[1]

THE SAVIOR'S TEACHINGS VERSUS THE DEVIL'S PLAYBOOK

The adversary tries to convince us to forget that blessings follow sacrifice. He seeks to stop our progress, and he will succeed if we succumb to his enticements, which inhibit our repentance. He has become ever more skillful in his attacks on the peace and joy of righteous living. In 2 Nephi 28:20–22, we read about our day and about the devil's offensive playbook against us.

Verse 20 reveals one strategy: "Behold, at that day shall he rage in the hearts of the children of men, and stir them up to anger against that which is good." The adversary uses discontentment and anger to stir up many feelings against good things. We can identify his anti-Christ teachings in this anger against foundational doctrines we hold dear. We encounter anger and discontent in every media messaging platform. Everywhere we look, we can see examples of people being stirred up in anger against good.

Another strategy is in verse 21: "Others will he pacify, and lull them away into carnal security, that they will say: All is well." We call this apathy. We recognize it in daily dialogue: "Why are you worried about that?" "It's not a big deal." "I don't care." "Whatever..." The devil loves us to feel apathy and say, "Oh, it doesn't really matter" or "What I do won't help much anyway."

Apathy destroys initiative. It kills the desire for work and knowledge. It extinguishes development and prosperity. It stops good people from being good examples and making a difference in the world. Apathy is dangerous and something to guard ourselves against. When we feel initiative and drive and motion, when we dream, when we feel hope, we guard against apathy.

A third strategy in the devil's playbook is in verse 22: "Others he flattereth away, and telleth them there is no hell; and he saith unto them: I am no devil, for there is none—and thus he whispereth in their ears, until he grasps them with his awful chains, from whence there is no deliverance."

In our day, I like to relate flattery to entitlement—a feeling and belief that we deserve something without working for it. The Spirit is offended by the idea that we deserve something or that we're entitled to something just by being alive or because we have achieved a certain status or acquired more than others. Such thinking denies the divinity within us, potentially making us merely comfort-seeking creatures. And so again, it's an anti-Christ attitude because it is contrary to what Christ taught when He said, in essence, "Here's your talent. Develop it. Make it more. Make it grow. Build my kingdom. Do something to show that you carry my light within you and that the world will be different because that light has shown through you."[2] People who feel entitled have difficulty showing the light of the Savior in their lives.

Nephi warns us that when the devil is successful with these strategies, he leads people "carefully down to hell."[3] However, when we know the devil's playbook, then we know what to guard against. The Savior has shown us the way we should live. His is a path of faith and hope and charity and a path of work and sacrifice. As we keep trying and doing our best, we have the Lord's promise, also recorded in 2 Nephi 28: "I will give unto the children of men line upon line, precept upon precept, here a little and there a little; and blessed are those who hearken unto my precepts, and lend an ear unto my counsel, for they shall learn wisdom; for unto him that receiveth I will give more."[4] The Savior offers hope even to those who have not yet hearkened to Him: "I will be merciful unto them, saith the Lord God, if they will repent and come unto me; for mine arm is lengthened out all the day long, saith the Lord of Hosts."[5]

His Spirit to Be with Us

Where do we gain strength to make the required sacrifices to succeed in our Heavenly Father's plan? How can we defend ourselves against the strategies of a determined adversary? How do we develop our own offense and receive the wisdom and learning the Lord promises us? Our great and empowering blessing is to receive the Holy Ghost and qualify for His constant companionship. It is through the Spirit that we learn precept upon precept and that we are warned and comforted.

Sister Eliza R. Snow said that the Holy Ghost "satisfies and fills up every longing of the human heart, and fills up every vacuum." Don't you love that? Sister Snow continued:

"When I am filled with that Spirit, my soul is satisfied, and I can say in good earnest, that the trifling things of the day do not seem to stand in my way at all. But just let me lose my hold of that spirit and power of the Gospel, and partake of the spirit of the world, in the slightest degree, and trouble comes; there is something wrong. I am tried, and what will comfort me? You cannot impart comfort to me that will satisfy the immortal mind, but that which comes from the Fountain above. And is it not our privilege to so live that we can have this constantly flowing into our souls?"[6]

If we want to have the Spirit "constantly flowing into our souls," we cannot neglect prayer. Prayer is free. It doesn't cost us anything. We don't have to go anywhere special to pray. Prayer can be with us and part of us always.

When prayer becomes a craving in our lives, when we breathe prayer, when we dream prayer, when we sigh prayer and cry prayer and love praying, then we begin to know some things about Heavenly Father and His Son and what They know about us and how much They love and trust us and how patient They are with us while we learn. Through that kind of prayer, we repent and feel the Lord's love around us.

To protect ourselves from adversarial influences and qualify for the companionship of the Spirit, we also cannot neglect spending time in the scriptures. When the scriptures become our friend, when they become our thesaurus and our dictionary, when they become our companion and our teacher, then the Lord can use them and open them for our benefit. We will find verses we didn't know existed, and we'll be blessed by words we are seeking.

Many years ago, I made a commitment to spend some time in the scriptures every day. At the time, I was wrestling with several scripture-reading goals. I was taking a religion class that required a certain amount of reading in the scriptures every day. Our Sunday School teacher had a planned course of scripture study for the year, our Relief Society presidency encouraged us to read in preparation for our lessons, I had my own lessons to prepare and teach, and our stake presidency announced a stakewide scripture-reading goal. I was listening in meetings to ward members tell of their own scripture-reading objectives. I was overwhelmed with all my scripture-study assignments and not measuring up in any of them. All those projects were well-intended, but I was feeling like a failure.

In my confusion and regret, I knelt down and made a promise to

Heavenly Father that I would spend some time in the scriptures every day for the rest of my life if He would please enlighten my mind and send peace to my soul. That was it: I promised to spend some time in the scriptures every day of my life. It was not a commitment to read a certain amount or follow a prescribed schedule. Since then, sometimes I read in the morning. Sometimes I read in the middle of the day. Sometimes I read at night, just before I fall asleep or as I'm falling asleep. Sometimes I have a glorious hour to spend in the scriptures, and sometimes I seize a moment in a frenzied day. Sometimes I read scriptures on my cell phone, and other times I am blessed to hold the books and look over past markings and learning. The words of the scriptures have become like the air I breathe. It seems as if it would be impossible to live without the "oxygen" I get from the scriptures.

PROMISES AND BLESSINGS

We need not fear or doubt if we guard against anger, apathy, and feelings of entitlement. If we follow the Savior's teachings, Satan will not overwhelm us. As we make prayer and scripture study a part of our life, every day, we will have the Spirit to guide us.

My Grandmother Duella's motto, "Let My Life Be Music," led her to a life filled with the Lord's guidance. She lived the principle of sacrifice in order to improve herself and serve others. She used her gift of music to lift and bless hundreds of people, and her influence continues today. She learned to diminish the influence of a determined adversary through inviting the Spirit into her life and home.

Making worthy sacrifices, large and small, will help us draw nearer to the Lord and prepare us to receive His greatest blessings. He has promised:

"After much tribulation come the blessings. Wherefore the day cometh that ye shall be crowned with much glory; the hour is not yet, but is nigh at hand.

"Remember this, which I tell you before, that you may lay it to heart, and receive that which is to follow."[7]

NOTES

1. Doctrine and Covenants 58:3–4.
2. See Matthew 25:14–30.
3. 2 Nephi 28:21.
4. 2 Nephi 28:30.
5. 2 Nephi 28:32.
6. Eliza R. Snow, "An Address by Miss Eliza R. Snow," *Millennial Star,* Jan. 13, 1874, 18; quoted in *Daughters in My Kingdom: The History and Work of Relief Society* (2011), 46.
7. Doctrine and Covenants 58:4–5.

14

WHAT IS OUR MISSION?

The lessons I learned from my parents have become part of my own reflections and now figure powerfully in my own teachings. The first chapter in this book began with the words of my mother, and it seems appropriate that this last chapter comprises lessons from my father. As Daddy approached his 92nd birthday, I could see his strong faith and luminous testimony shining ever brighter from his weakening physical body. One evening I stopped by my parents' home after a day of meetings at Church headquarters. Daddy was dozing on the bed, and he had difficulty rousing himself to carry on a conversation. After about an hour watching him rest, I left to go home. As I was opening the back door, Daddy called out to me, "Come back! Come back!" He was suddenly awake, and he had something to say. He started to reflect on his life, and his words were profound. I grabbed any scraps of paper I could find—receipts, reminder notes, napkins, tissues—and I wrote, as fast as I could, the words he spoke. They were the words of a patriarch to his family. I typed them as soon as I returned home. Only a few weeks later, on April 24, 2010, I spoke at his funeral and shared the substance of his reflections—about our identity, purpose, and work in the house of Israel and about the joy of keeping covenants.

My father, William Grant Bangerter, loved purposeful gatherings. He enjoyed the renewal of faith and eternal friendship at such events. He never stopped gathering with his mission companions and his own missionaries, and he presided over many family gatherings every year. He was happiest when celebrating mission calls, temple marriages, and new babies and when he was hosting parties at the farm in Alpine and camping with us in the High Uinta Mountains.

When I was a little girl, every night Daddy was home was family night. That means we usually enjoyed more than one family home evening a week. Before bedtime, he and Mama prayed with us, unfolded the scriptures to us, read favorite books aloud to us, and sang songs with us. We sang folk songs in various languages, silly songs, and hymns. Their purpose in moving to their farm in Alpine was to provide a gathering place for their family. It was there that they gathered us for cookouts, work parties, horse rides, and family councils. Family nights and gatherings with my parents continued throughout their lives.

For Daddy, the significance of gathering was based on his deep understanding of the gospel of Jesus Christ and our responsibilities in the house of Israel. No one understood priesthood and eternal families better than he did. No one understood their eternal mission and purpose on the earth better than he did.

Just before Daddy died, we gathered on the Sunday evening following general conference, as was our tradition, to review conference. At that time, he said: "It is extremely remarkable that each one of you gives a short report and in every case you bring up something that I missed in conference. I am so grateful for our family, that you have taken time to understand what was there. I ask that you all be blessed."

At that same family gathering, he taught us his final sermon, saying: "I have had an impression, and I think very deeply of the mission we have to serve before the Lord and how we have been called by the vision of prophets. The vision of the house of Israel is laid upon us. I ask you to look at the families around us and see them exploding and blossoming and with every possibility of being brought up with knowledge and truth. There are certain blessings that pertain to every one of us. Baptism, then the Holy Ghost. As the young men grew, they received the blessings of the priesthood. Then as they grew, they went to the temple. I emphasize that none of you who are married went to the temple in this condition by yourselves, but with your companion. You have organized with your companion an eternal family—and beyond that come the grandchildren, and beyond that the vision of what else is ahead. So we see the fulfillment of the promise that the work of the kingdom and the house of Israel is in full effect."

A PRIVATE CONVERSATION WITH MY FATHER

Only a few days earlier, Daddy and I had spent a quiet hour together. He spoke as a true patriarch should and asked me, "What is your mission? What is my mission? Why are we on the earth? We are here to develop ourselves and build the kingdom of God!" He said that an impressive career is an interesting experience, but serving in Church leadership is something very special. He spoke of having been called into the Lord's service and asked again, "What is our mission? Why did Heavenly Father send me forth to this service? I was not sent on earth to be a farmer or carpenter. I was sent to serve and respond where I was sent and be carried around the world in the Lord's service. There is a difference in what we choose to devote our lives to. Taking care of our posterity takes precedence over all other things. Do you see the panorama of this family? Think of the achievement and purpose our family has come to the earth to perform. The vision of our family is the vision of our purpose before the Lord." Daddy then talked about his children, their earthly missions, and how he has seen their missions unfolding.

After that, he spoke at length about Mother and her mission. She was a single woman of great ability when she met my father, who was a faithful man of God, a bishop with three children who had lost his wife. When they met, Mother was within weeks of leaving for New York City to pursue a graduate degree at Columbia University. As they began dating, Mama could feel that her life's mission was going to change. Although Daddy was very willing to wait for her to complete her goal, she tried to imagine ten months away from him and the children. She thought, "Who is going to take care of those children while I'm gone for ten months? They need me now!" And from that point, she said goodbye to Columbia in her heart and mind.[1]

As I talked with Daddy before he died, he reflected on Mother's willingness to forego her graduate degree. "Her mission was not to go to Columbia," he said, with gratitude. "It was known and directed in the heavens that only Mother could help me carry what I had to carry, and only she could bring forth this family."

Continuing, he said, "Mother grows more wonderful to me every day. What a mission she has fulfilled and is even now carrying out! She has lived a life of true nobility. She was called to be the wife of a humble bishop, and she woke up to great leadership. She was called to be a mother to share the gospel with rejoicing and happiness."

He added, "Heavenly Father sent us here to live, learn, perform in the midst of trials, and, when we're finished, be united with our companions and move forward to eternal life with countless members of our posterity."

Daddy and Mama were a great and remarkable team. They planned together and executed their inspired plans for their family. Daddy had absolute confidence and trust in Mother and was amazed at her accomplishments. In their later years, he couldn't express strongly enough how remarkable she was and what a gift he was blessed with when he found her. Their example was the perfect model of a mother and a father leading together.

COVENANT KEEPERS AND FRIENDS OF GOD

My father was wise, scholarly, and erudite. He was humble and submissive. He was a teacher of truth, a builder of men, and a friend of God. As he adored his family, he thrived on Church service and the work of the Lord. It put a smile on his face and a spring in his step. He was willing to put forth the spiritual effort to receive revelation and wait for it to come.

He taught that "the Saints of God are committed to wear out their lives . . . in carrying the gospel to all the world, to strengthen those who falter, and to bring forth the salvation of those who have passed beyond without the blessings of the priesthood" and that "receiving the fullness of the priesthood makes the Saints capable of living with and presiding over their posterity in an eternal union of ever-expanding power in the wonderful time ahead."[2]

My mother was a woman with a "mother heart." She believed that if she had the Spirit with her, she could "speak with the tongue of angels."[3] She had a great vision of her own potential and implicit confidence in the promise in all God's children. She had an optimistic, can-do attitude. Her life was governed by a few simple adages: "Every person has five or six geniuses." "Children are people." "Love people for their differences."[4] She wrote:

"Many times I look back at my life experiences and say, 'Well wasn't that lucky,' or, 'Aren't I blessed;' but really, it was the Lord leading me and guiding me. . . . Recognizing the Lord's hand in my life has helped me realize that NOTHING was happenstance. It wasn't coincidence that I met Grant before going to Columbia University. . . . The Lord had His hand in our lives every moment. We were led every moment, and it was miraculous."[5]

Shortly before Daddy passed away, he was asked to speak in stake conference. He quoted a scripture passage that, for me, is a testimony of his faith in God and His promises:

"I, the Lord, am merciful and gracious unto those who fear me, and delight to honor those who serve me in righteousness and in truth unto the end.

"Great shall be their reward and eternal shall be their glory. . . .

"Yea, even the wonders of eternity shall they know, and things to come will I show them, even the things of many generations."[6]

How blessed I am to have been taught by parents who love the Lord. Through faithfulness in keeping God's covenants, they became His precious fruit. From them I learned of my eternal identity, purpose, and mission. Their testimonies of those truths ran deep in their souls, enabling them and their posterity to live by their motto: "Enjoy it!"

NOTES

1. Geraldine Hamblin Bangerter, in Heidi Beck Shin, *Welcome the Task: The Biography of Geraldine Hamblin Bangerter* (2013), 66.
2. William Grant Bangerter, *The Collected Works of William Grant Bangerter* (2008), 462–63; capitalization standardized.
3. 2 Nephi 31:13; 32:2.
4. Geraldine Hamblin Bangerter, in *Welcome the Task,* 270–71.
5. Geraldine Hamblin Bangerter, in *Welcome the Task,* 266.
6. Doctrine and Covenants 76:5–6, 8.

INDEX

Abraham, 12–13, 32–35

Abrahamic covenant, 12–14, 33–35

Adam and Eve, 64–65, 91, 101–8

Adversity, triumph over, 105. *See also* Trials

Agency, 106, 122–23

Alma, 56–57, 94–95

Ancient fathers and mothers, 32–33, 91–93

Anger, 150

Apathy, 150–51

Apostles, 38, 40

Astronomy, 82–83

Atonement, 36–38, 105

Ballard, Melvin J., 20–21, 28, 29

Ballard, M. Russell, 39

Bangerter, Frederick, 86

Bangerter, Geraldine Hamblin: spirit of enjoyment of, 3–9; service rendered by, 24–25, 111–13; attends São Paulo Temple rededication, 28; sets family goals, 65–66, 106–7; love of, of music, 147; life mission of, 159–60; faith of, 160–61

Bangerter, Glenda, 66–67, 69

Bangerter, Maria, 86

Bangerter, Peggy Brasilia, 5

Bangerter, William Grant: spirit of enjoyment of, 3–9; and knowing identity as child of God, 10–11; called to Brazilian Mission, 21–22; presides over Brazilian Mission, 22–26; and construction of São Paulo Temple, 27–28; attends São Paulo Temple rededication, 28; sets family goals, 65–66, 106–7; on purpose of mortality, 78; service rendered by, 111; and organization of Church in Brazil, 127; teachings of, 156–61

Baptism, 37

Bawden, Ann, 86

Bawden, Henry, 86

Bawden, John Howard, 21

Beck, J. Paul, 93–95, 107

Beck, June Strong, 93–95

Beck, Ramon, 68–69, 70, 72

Benson, Ezra Taft, 23, 53

Bishops, 130–31, 133–34

Blazer Scouts, 111–13

Blessings, following trials, 150, 154–55

Book of Mormon, 34, 35–36

Boy Scouts, 111–13

Brands, 47

Brazil: author's memories of, 18, 19; Restoration of gospel in, 19–21, 29; construction of São Paulo Temple in, 27–28; author returns to, 28–29

Brazilian Mission: attitude of enjoyment in, 4–7; William Bangerter called to, 21–23; William Bangerter called as president of, 21–24; Geraldine Bangerter's service in, 24–25; progress in, 25–26; organization of, 127–28

Brigham Young University, 68–72

Brotherhood, 138–41

Brown, Hugh B., 23

Cars, old, 111

Children: teaching, 14–15; and commandment to multiply, 103–4; music taught to, 148–50

Children of God, knowing our identity as, 10–16

Christofferson, D. Todd, 136–37

Chronic illness, 116–18

Church history, 47–48

Church leaders, sustaining, 130–31

Commandment, to be fruitful and multiply, 101–8

Confirmation, 37–38

Covenant family: allegory concerning, 7–8; knowing our identity as members of, 10–16

Covenant(s): keeping, 7–9, 103; restoration of, 40; purpose of, 78–79; and faith of pioneers, 85–89; salvation through, 107–8

Cowdery, Oliver, 12

Daughters in My Kingdom: The History and Work of Relief Society: assignment regarding, 43; instructions regarding, 44; and myths about Relief Society and LDS women, 45–46; and purpose of Relief Society, 46–48; research for, 46–48; creation of, 49–52; lessons of, 53–55; impact of, 55–57; as spiritual record, 55–57; and responsibilities of quorums and Relief Society, 140

Death, 76–77, 79–80

Discipleship, 113–15

Discontentment, 150

Dixie College, 66–68

Doctrine and Covenants, 34

Dominion, 105

Dress and keep, 106

Education: as family goal, 65–66; at Dixie College, 66–68; at BYU, 68–72; lessons learned through, 72–75. *See also* Knowledge; Learning

Elias, 13

Elijah, 90, 91, 93

Empowerment, through Holy Ghost, 152–54

Enjoyment, spirit of, 6–9, 74, 161

Entitlement, 151

Eternal life, 90

Eve, 64–65, 101–8

Experience, learning from: and purpose of mortality, 63–65; and higher education as family goal, 65–66; at Dixie College, 66–68; at BYU, 68–72; lessons gleaned from, 72–75

Eyre, George, 86

Eyre, Rebecca, 86

Eyring, Henry B., 134–35

Faith: learning through, 83–85; and covenants of pioneers, 85–89; developing, 93–95; through Holy Ghost, 95–97; of Adam and Eve, 101–8; and subduing negative thoughts and influences, 104–5; and revelation, 119–20

Family: happiness in, 80; teaching and leading in, 106–7; priesthood quorums and Relief Society as support for, 137–39; missions of, 157–60

Family goals, 65–66, 106–7

Family history work, 14, 85–89

Family home evening, 157

Fellowship, 136–37

Flattery, 151

Fruitful life, 101–8

Fundamental truths, 31–40

Gathering of Israel, 16, 18–29, 32–35

Gatherings, 157

Genealogy, 14, 85–89

General conference, 157

"Gentleman-Rankers" (Kipling), 10

Goal(s): for family, 65–66, 106–7; completing, 72–73; focusing on, 74

Goates, George, 136–7

God: relying on, 75; knows His children, 110–15

Good Samaritan, 113

Gospel, restoration of, 19–21, 29, 31–40, 84, 114

Hamblin, Daphne, 86

Hamblin, Duella Eyre, 146–47, 148–50, 154–55

Hamblin, Jacob, 86, 96–97

Hamblin, Marcene, 146, 149

Hamblin, Mary Ann, 86

Hamblin, Oscar, 86

Happiness, 74

Help, 73–74, 110–15

Hepatitis, 25

Higher education: as family goal, 65–66; at Dixie College, 66–68; at BYU, 68–72; lessons learned through, 72–75. See also Knowledge; Learning

Hinckley, Gordon B., 44, 54, 139–40

Holy Ghost: gift of, 37–38; seeking, 74–75; faith through, 95–97; revelation through, 118, 119–20, 123; recognizing, 120–21; empowerment through, 152–54

Hope, 83–85

Hunter, Howard W., 54

Identity, knowing, 10–16

Illness, 25, 116–18

Inertia, 72–73

INDEX

Israel: responsibilities of, 14–15; gathering of, 16, 18–29, 32–35; work of house of, 157–58

Jack, Elaine L., 37
Jacob 5, 7–8
Jesus Christ: depending on, 16; and Abrahamic covenant, 33–34; Book of Mormon as witness of, 35–36; baptism of, 37; female disciples of, 46–48; relying on, 75; salvation through, 78; faith in, 105; following example of, 151–52

Kimball, Spencer W., 23, 27, 54, 57, 128, 135
Kipling, Rudyard, 10
Kirtland Temple, 12, 106
Knowledge: thirst for, 74; spiritual, 104–5. See also Higher education; Learning
Korihor, 11

Learning: through science, 82–83; through hope and faith, 83–85; replenishment through, 104. See also Higher education; Knowledge
Lee, Harold B., 23, 139
Love, of God, 110–15
Lyman, Amy Brown, 53
Lyman, Wyoming, 85–86

Maxwell, Neal A., 122
McConkie, Bruce R., 122–23, 134
McKay, David O., 129
Metropolitan Museum of Art, 91
Ministering, 134–39
Missionary work: as responsibility of House of Israel, 14–15; Brazilian Saints called to, 28–29; and

gathering of Israel, 32–35; of Apostles, 38; in spirit world, 79–80
Monson, Thomas S., 22, 77, 134–35, 136
Mortality: purpose of, 63–65, 78–79, 158–59; in plan of salvation, 77–78; evaluating our time in, 79–80; perilous times in, 136
Motivation, 72–73
Movement, 72–73
Multiplying, commandment concerning, 103–4
Music, 145–52, 154–55
Music books, 145

Nehor, 10–11
Nelson, Russell M., 8
New skills, developing, 74

Oaks, Dallin H., 39, 136
Obedience, 107–8, 119–20
Old cars, 111
Ordinances, 36–38, 107–8

Packer, Boyd K., 48, 54, 128, 129, 136, 140
Parable(s): of talents, 103–4; of good Samaritan, 113
Patience, 123–24
Patriarchal blessing, 34
Peace, 122–23
Perilous times, 137
Peter, 24, 34, 95–96
Peterson, Tadd, 52
Piano, 146, 148–50
Pioneers, 85–89
Planetarium, 82–83
Plan of salvation, 77–78
Planting, 93–95

Pratt, Parley P., 20
Prayer, 22–23, 152–54
Pre-earth life, 77–78
Priesthood: power through ordinances of, 36–38; authority and keys of, 38–40; restoration of, 40, 90–91; women's access to blessings of, 53–54; promises administered by, 92–93; patterns of, 129–31
Priesthood quorums: changes made to, 126–27; in Brazilian Mission, 127; defined, 127–28; purpose of, 128; reasons for organization into, 126–41; responsibilities and promise regarding, 139–41
Priorities, 73
Procreation, 103–4
Promises, 89–93
Prophet, 40

Questions, right, 123
Quorums. *See* Priesthood quorums

Relationships, 80
Relief Society: in Brazilian Mission, 24–25, 27–28; myths regarding LDS women and, 45–46; purpose of, 48–49, 128–29; changes made to, 126–27; organization of, 127–28; defined, 128–29; reasons for organization into, 126–41; responsibilities and promise regarding, 139–41. See also *Daughters in My Kingdom: The History and Work of Relief Society*
Repentance, 119
Replenish, 104
Restoration of gospel, 19–20, 29, 31–40, 84, 114

Revelation, 116–18; what it is, 118; climate for, 119–20; recognizing, 120–21; what it is not, 121; working to receive, 121–22; agency and, 122–23; asking right questions for, 123; patience in receiving, 123–24; and priesthood patterns, 131
Richards, Stephen L, 4
Right questions, for revelation, 123
Rollins, Caroline, 85
Rollins, Evaline Walker, 85–86, 88
Rollins, James Henry, 85–86
Rollins, Mary Elizabeth, 85

Sacrament, 37–38, 104
Sacrifices, 107–8, 146–47, 148, 154–55
Salvation, 77–78, 107–8, 131–33
São Paulo Temple, 27–28
Sarah, 12–13, 33
Satan, 96, 121–22, 150–52
Science, 82–83
Scriptures, 22, 153–54. *See also* Book of Mormon; Doctrine and Covenants
Sealing power, 90–91
Sea of Galilee, 123–24
Seed, faith compared to, 94–95
Self-reliance, 132–34
Service, 110–15, 139–40, 146–47, 154–55
Shin, Samuel InJae, 76
Sisterhood, 137–39
Skills, developing, 74
Smith, George Albert, 54
Smith, Joseph: Elias appears to, 12–13; on Church growth, 29; and faith of pioneers, 87–88; and restoration

of priesthood, 90–91; service rendered by, 114; and organization of Relief Society, 127–28, 131, 138
Smith, Joseph F., 38, 54, 128
Smith, Joseph Fielding, 13, 23, 53
Snow, Eliza R., 49, 53, 56, 138, 152
"Somebody," 110, 111, 113–15
Spiritual knowledge, 104–5
Spirit world, 79–80
Stewardship, 106
Storehouse, 132–33
Subdue, 104–5
Sugar beets, 136–37
Support, in quorums and Relief Society, 137–39
Sustaining leaders, 130–31

Talents, parale of, 103–4
Tanner, Susan Winder, 50–51
Teamwork, 72–75

Temple and temple ordinances, 14–15, 38
Testimony, creation of, 83–85, 117–18
Trials, 4–7, 137, 149–50, 154–55. *See also* Adversity, triumph over
Truth, 31–40
Tuttle, A. Theodore, 23

Walkenhorst, Nicole Erickson, 51
Walmsley, Elizabeth, 87
Wards, 130–31
West, Aaron, 51
Whitney, Elizabeth Ann, 120
Widtsoe, John A., 132
Women: access of, to priesthood, 39, 53–54; identity and purpose of, 44–46; and research for *Daughters in My Kingdom*, 46–48
Wood, William, 87
Work, 65–66